animal knits

animal knits

25 fun handknits for children and toddlers

Zoë Mellor

Trafalgar Square Publishing

To Toby Tiger, my son, who is
great fun and animal mad

First published in the United States of America in 2001 by
Trafalgar Square Publishing, North Pomfret, Vermont 05053

1 2 3 4 5 6 7 8 9

ISBN 1-57076-191-4

Library of Congress Catalog Number 00-108780

EDITOR: Kate Haxell
ART EDITOR: Luise Roberts
PHOTOGRAPHY: Joey Toller
STYLING: Zoë Mellor
PATTERN CHECKERS: Eva Yates, Gill Everett

Reproduction in Singapore by Classic Scan

contents

The page numbers in bold refer to the colour photograph and
those in roman to the pattern page

introduction

I have recently opened a small shop in Brighton, selling both knitwear and my range of fleece garments and accessories, so life is rather busy. However, I really love inventing new knitwear designs and choosing colours to make them in. Designing all the animal knits for this book has been great fun and I hope that you will enjoy knitting them as much as I enjoyed creating them.

There are 26 designs for babies and children up to 6 years old to choose from in this book, ranging from funky cow-print and tiger-stripe patterned garments to contemporary versions of classic Fair Isle designs. I have designed a collection of sweaters, jackets, hats, scarves, bootees, bags, cushions, blankets and two knitted toys – so I hope that there is something to appeal to everyone.

I have some personal favourites from the collection: the sweet baby bootees (page 10), the bold and bright butterfly sweater (page 20), and the ladybird hat (page 48), are three designs that I particularly like. I also loved the cushions (pages 15 and 46), so much that they are now have permanent places on my sofa. Toby, my two-year-old son, is mad about animals, particularly cows, so his favourites are the cow-print scarf and hat (page 41), and the cow-print jacket (page 42). Choose your own favourites, or let the special little people in your life choose theirs – and Happy Knitting!

Zoë Mellor

b u n n y j a c k e t

There are lots of different textures in this jacket: stocking stitch, cables, a moss-stitch collar and cuffs and a pretty pointed edge. Add the Fair Isle bands and bunny motifs and this jacket will delight knitters and little girls alike.

PATTERN PAGE 49–50

animal bootees

One little bunny said to one little bear, 'What are you doing, standing over there.'

'I'm playing with my brother, he's over here too. He's the other cuddly, snuggly, smiley bear shoe.'

PATTERNS PAGE 51

sheep jacket

Traditional Fair Isle bands are given a contemporary twist by working them in bright, fresh hues. The woolly sheep border incorporates two practical pockets for a truly versatile jacket.

PATTERN PAGE 52-53

a n i m a l
b l a n k e t

This blanket is knitted in
separate squares, so it is an
easy project for a beginner to
make. The animal patches are
alternated with simple moss-
stitch squares.

PATTERN PAGE 54–55

The fluffy chenille chicken at the centre is surrounded by other farmyard animals, and the farmer and his wife. The bright colours and bold shapes will make this cushion a favourite of young and old alike.

farmyard
cushion

PATTERN PAGE 56-57

camel waistcoat

This waistcoat was inspired by Turkish rug designs. The striped back, with its single motif and patterned border, contrasts well with the patterned front. The moss-stitch button bands and border add texture to complement the intarsia knitting.

PATTERN PAGE 58–59

butterflies and birds
jacket

Worked in soft tones, this pretty jacket
will look good with jeans for every day,
or over a favourite skirt or dress
for special occasions.

PATTERN PAGE 60–61

This bold and bright butterfly
sweater is worked in chunky cotton
yarn, so it's great for the summer.
The sleeves and back are
plain, apart from the borders,
so it is easy to knit, too.

butterfly sweater

PATTERN PAGE 62–63

dog sweater

This spotty dog sweater is suitable for both boys and girls.

Simple stripes on the sleeves complement the central motif and

the contrast cast-off edge gives a twist to the classic rib.

PATTERN PAGE 64–65

Texture and tone are combined in this practical backpack for boys and girls. The golden lion has a soft chenille mane, which stands out from the bright cotton yarns used for the rest of the bag.

lion rucksack

PATTERN PAGE 66

Easy and quick to knit, this simple
bag will hold toys, school books or
supplies for a day out with ease. A
recommended length for the strap
is given, but this can be adjusted
to suit absolutely anyone.

elephant bag

PATTERN PAGE 67

elephant jacket

Elephants are always popular with children, so this jacket is sure to
appeal to boys and girls alike. The simple garter-stitch collar, buttonbands
and hem are knitted in a contrast colour for a contemporary look.

PATTERN PAGE 68–70

tiger-stripe
jacket

This jacket, with its bold tiger stripes, is perfect for children who are wild at heart! It is funky and fashionable and might well find its way into older children's wardrobes as well.

PATTERN PAGE 71-72

farm sweater

Bright, punchy colours and the simple graphic shapes of farmyard animals

will make this sweater a firm favourite. The pointed hem and wide neck and wristbands,

all knitted in bright red, set off the motifs perfectly.

PATTERN PAGE 73–75

t o y
r a b b i t

This loveable bunny has big floppy ears and a huggable body. She is easy to knit and will be adored by children and adults alike.

PATTERN PAGE 76–77

toy dog

As he is knitted in one piece, this little spotty dog

is really easy to make. This is a project that children could

try as it is so much fun and the result is great.

PATTERN PAGE 78

duck jacket

A modern classic, this pretty jacket has a lacy edge with a border of marching ducks.

The daisies are placed randomly, so you can have as many or as few as you wish. Finish

the jacket with mother-of-pearl buttons for a co-ordinated look.

PATTERN PAGE 79–80

tiger sweater

Turquoise, lime green and orange combine to give a really modern twist to a classically styled sweater. The leaping tiger motif makes this the perfect garment for all little explorers.

PATTERN PAGE 81–82

This vibrant jacket has bands of little fish swimming around it: perfect for a day out at the seaside. The simple shape and geometric patterning make it suitable for both boys and girls.

fish jacket

PATTERN PAGE 83–84

f i s h   h a t

This hat is sure to turn heads! Make it
to go with the fish jacket (page 38) or
just on its own. It is knitted in chunky
cotton, so it isn't itchy, and the earflaps
will keep out the cold.

PATTERN PAGE 85–86

cow-print
scarf and
hat

This bold duo are just great for

the cold weather. Finished in moss

stitch, they are very fashionable

as well as playful.

PATTERN PAGE 87

cow-print jacket

Simply stylish, this eyecatching jacket is also

easy to knit and practical to wear. It is sure to be

loved by cowboys and cowgirls alike!

PATTERN PAGE 88–89

This cheerful rooster will make
every morning brighter, no matter
what the weather. The simple
rolled edges in a contrast colour
make it a great sweater for
little snappy dressers.

rooster sweater

PATTERN PAGE 90-91

ladybird
cushion and blanket

This baby cushion and blanket are brilliant for any new arrival.

Breaking away from the traditional pastel baby colours,

they are simple and stylish for the modern baby.

PATTERNS PAGES 92-93

ladybird hat

Generously sized to keep little ears warm, the bright colours

and perky antenna on this hat make it another

garment that is perfect for boys and girls.

PATTERNS PAGE 94

bunny jacket

TENSION (GAUGE)
20sts and 28 rows = 10cm (4in) square over stocking (stockinette) stitch using 4mm (US 6) needles.

ABBREVIATIONS
See page 95 and

c4b = place the next 2sts on cable needle. leave at back of work, k2, k2 from cable needle.

BACK
Using 4mm (US 6) needles and light pink, cast on 61(65:71)sts. Working in stocking (stockinette) stitch, follow graph, (24 rows). Change to M and work as folls:–

ROW 25: knit.

ROW 26: p4(6:9) * k1 p1 inc p1 k1 p7 * four times, k1 p1 inc p1 k1 p4(6:9). *(66:70:76sts)*

ROW 27: k4(6:9) * p1 k4 p1 k7 * 4 times, p1 k4 p1 k4(6:9).

ROW 28: p4(6:9) * k1 p4 k1 p7 * 4 times, k1 p4 k1 p4(6:9).

ROW 29: k4(6:9) * p1 c4b p1 k7 * 4 times, p1 c4b p1 k4(6:9).

ROW 30: as row 28.

Repeat rows 27–30 to completion of row 71(79:89).

Shape neck: WS facing, patt 24(25:26), cast off 18(20:24)sts, patt 24(25:26).

On 24(26:26)sts, dec neck edge on next 2 rows. Cast (bind) off.

Rejoin yarn to remaining sts and work to match.

LEFT FRONT
Using 4mm (US 6) needles and light pink, cast on 30 (32:35)sts. Working in stocking (stockinette) stitch, follow graph.

Change to M and work as folls:–

ROW 25: knit.

ROW 26: p9 * k1 p1 inc p1 k1* p7 * to * again, p4(6:9). *(32:34:37sts)*

ROW 27: k4(6:9) p1 k4 p1 k7 p1 k4 p1 k9.

ROW 28: p9 k1 p4 k1 p7 k1 p4 k1 p4(6:9).

ROW 29: k4(6:9) p1 c4b p1 k7 p1 c4b p1 k9.

ROW 30: as row 28.

Repeat rows 27–30 to completion of row 63(69:79).

SIZES

SIZES	1	2	3
to fit years	6mths–1	1–2	2–3
chest actual cm(in)	61(24)	66(26)	71(28)
back length cm(in)	29(11½)	32(12½)	36(14)
sleeve seam cm(in)	18(7)	20(8)	25(10)

MATERIALS
Rowan Handknit DK Cotton 50g balls

	1	2	3
dark pink (M)	6	6	7
light pink	1	1	1
ecru	1	1	1

5 buttons

1 pair 3¼mm (US 3) and 4mm (US 6) needles
Cable needle

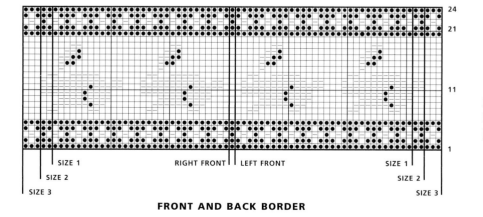

- □ DARK PINK (M)
- ● LIGHT PINK
- ⊟ ECRU

| 24 |
| 21 |
| 11 |
| 1 |

SIZE 1   RIGHT FRONT | LEFT FRONT   SIZE 1

SIZE 2   SIZE 2

SIZE 3   SIZE 3

FRONT AND BACK BORDER

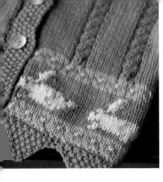

bunny jacket

** **Shape neck:** WS facing, cast (bind) off 4(5:6)sts, patt to end.
Dec neck edge on next 6(6:7) rows.
(22:23:24sts)
Work to completion of row 74(82:92).
Cast (bind) off.**

RIGHT FRONT

As left front to completion of row 24.
Change to M and work as folls:–
ROW 25: knit.
ROW 26: p4(6:9) * k1 p1 inc p1 k1* p7,
* to * again, p9.
ROW 27: k9 p1 k4 p1 k7 p1 k4 p1 k4(6:9).
Row 27 sets cable patt as on left front. Cont in patt to completion of row 64(70:80).
Starting RS facing, work neck ** to ** as left front.

SLEEVES

Using 3¼mm (US 3) needles and M, cast on 33(35:37)sts and work 8 rows of moss stitch, (every row, * k1 p1* to last st, k1).
Change to 4mm (US 6) needles and stocking (stockinette) stitch. Work rows 1–5 of graph, inc each end of row 3. Change to M.
ROW 6: purl.
ROW 7: k15(16:17) p1 k1 inc k1 p1 k15(16:17).
ROW 8: p15(16:17) k1 p4 k1 p15(16:17).
ROW 9: inc, k14(15:16) p1 c4b p1 k14(15:16) inc.
ROW 10: p16(17:18) k1 p4 k1 p16(17:18).
Cont cable and inc each end of every 4 rows to 54(58:64)sts. Cont without shaping until work measures 18(20:25)cm (7:8:10in).
Cast (bind) off.

EDGING

Using 3¼mm (US 3) needles and M, cast on 2sts.
ROW 1: k2.
ROW 2: inc, k1.
ROW 3: k1 p1 inc.
ROW 4: inc, k1 p1 k1.
ROWS 5–8: moss stitch, inc at shaped edge on every row. *(9sts)*
ROW 9: moss stitch.
ROWS 10–16: dec at shaped edge on each row, moss stitch. *(2sts)*
Repeat rows 1–16 until straight edge fits lower edge of garment, ending after a complete patt repeat.

BUTTONBAND

Using 3¼mm (US 3) needles and M, cast on 6sts and work in moss stitch until band, when slightly stretched, fits front to neck shaping. Cast (bind) off. Sew into place.
Mark positions for 5 buttons, the first and last 1cm (½in) from top and bottom edges and remaining 3 evenly spaced between.

BUTTONHOLE BAND

Work to match buttonband making buttonholes to match button positions by: moss 2, k2tog, yrn, moss 2.

COLLAR

Join shoulder seams. Using 3¼mm (US 3) needles and M, with right side facing and beginning and ending at centre of front bands, pick up and knit 67(73:77)sts from neck. Work as folls:–
ROWS 1–2: k2, moss to last 2sts, k2.
ROW 3: k2, moss to last 3sts, inc, k2.
Repeat row 3 until collar measures 6cm (2¾in). Cast (bind) off loosely in moss stitch.

MAKING UP

Measure 12(13:14)cm (4¾:5:5½in) down from shoulder seam, place pin. Set in sleeves between pins and stitch. Join sleeve and side seams. Weave in any loose ends. Attach edging to garment, omitting front bands. Sew on buttons.

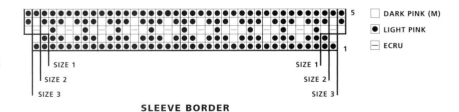

SLEEVE BORDER

☐ DARK PINK (M)
● LIGHT PINK
⊟ ECRU

animal bootees

TENSION (GAUGE)
32sts and 40 rows = 10cm (4in) square over stocking (stockinette) stitch using 3mm (US 3) needles.

ABBREVIATIONS
See page 95.

SOLE
Using 3mm (US 3) needles and A, cast on 53sts.
ROW 1: ✳ inc, k24, inc ✳ twice, k1.
ROW 2–4: knit.
ROW 5: ✳ inc, k26, inc ✳ twice, k1.
ROWS 6–8: knit.
ROW 9: ✳ inc, k28, inc ✳ twice, k1.
ROW 10: knit.

EDGING
Work picot edge as folls:–
Change to C.
ROW 1: knit.
ROW 2: purl.
ROW 3: k1, ✳ yrn k2tog ✳ to end.
ROW 4: purl.
ROWS 5–6: as rows 1–2.
Change to B.
ROW 7: fold work at row of holes and knit together, 1st from needle and 1st from FIRST row of picot, all across row.
ROWS 8–20: knit.

FOOT
Shape foot as folls:–
ROW 1: k36 k2tog, turn.
ROW 2: k8 s1 k1 psso, turn.
ROW 3: k8 k2tog, turn.
ROWS 4–23: as rows 2–3 ten times. *(41sts)*
ROW 24: as row 2.
ROWS 25–28: knit across all sts.
Change to A and knit 1 row.
Change to k1 p1 rib and work 27 rows.
Change to C.
ROW 29: purl.
ROW 30: cast (bind) off knitwise
Make second bootee to match.

EARS
Bunny ears
Using B, cast on 8sts. Work 23 rows in stocking (stockinette) stitch, dec each end of rows 15, 19 and 23. Change to A and work 23 rows in stocking (stockinette) stitch (starting with a purl row), inc each end of rows 2, 4 and 8. Cast (bind) off.
Make three more ears to match.

Teddy ears
Using B, cast on 8sts. Work 7 rows in stocking (stockinette) stitch, dec each end of rows 6 and 7. Change to C and work 7 rows in stocking (stockinette) stitch (starting with a purl row), inc each end of rows 2 and 3. Cast (bind) off.
Make three more ears to match.

MAKING UP.
Join ear side seams. Join foot, heel and back of ankle with a flat seam. Attach base of ears to bootees (see photograph). Embroider faces using brown.

SIZE
to fit	6–9 mths

MATERIALS
Jaeger Merino 50g balls
Bunny bootees

light pink (A)	1
cream (B)	1
dark pink (C)	1
small amount of **brown**	

Teddy bootees

cream (A)	1
beige (B)	1
brown (C)	1

1 pair 3mm (US 3) needles

sheep jacket

TENSION (GAUGE)
22sts and 28 rows = 10cm (4in) square over stocking (stockinette) stitch using 4mm (US 6) needles.

ABBREVIATIONS
See page 95.

BACK
Using 4mm (US 6) needles and C, cast on 75(87:93)sts. Using stocking (stockinette) stitch, work rows 1–30 from graph.
Change to stripe patt and work as follows:–

ROWS 31–33: C
ROW 34: B
ROW 35: 3(3:1)B * 1F 3B * to last 0(0:1)st, 0(0:1)B
ROW 36: * 1F 1C * to last st, 1F
ROW 37: as row 35
ROW 38: B
ROWS 39–42: D
ROW 43: M
ROW 44: 3(3:1)M * 1A 3M * to last 0(0:1)st, 0(0:1)M

ROW 45: * 1A 1B * to last st, 1A
ROW 46: as row 44
ROW 47: M
ROWS 48–51: F
ROW 52: E
ROW 53: 3(3:1)E * 1B 3E * to last 0(0:1)st, 0(0:1)E
ROW 54: * 1B 1D * to last st, 1B
ROW 55: as row 53
ROW 56: E
Rows 31–56 form stripe patt. Cont in patt working shapings as folls:

Armhole
ROWS 57–58(67–68:77–78): cast off 4(5:6)sts, patt to end

Shoulders and neck
ROW 88(102:118): patt 21(25:26), cast (bind) off 25(27:29)sts, patt 21(25:26)
On 21(25:26)sts, dec neck edge on next 2 rows. Cast (bind) off.
Rejoin yarns to remaining sts at neck edge and work to match.

POCKETS (2)
Using 4mm (US 6) needles and M, cast on 26sts and work 26 rows in stocking (stockinette) stitch.
Leave on holder.

LEFT FRONT
Using 4mm (US 6) needles and C, cast on 37(43:46)sts. Using stocking (stockinette) stitch, work rows 1–30 from graph.
Change to stripe patt as on back noting
ROW 31: place pocket: using C k5(11:14), place next 26sts on holder, knit 26sts from pocket, k6
ROW 35: 2(0:2)B * 1F 3B *, ending last rep 2B
ROW 36: * 1C 1F * to last st, 1C

Armhole
ROW 57(67:77): cast off 4(5:6)sts, patt to end

Neck
ROW 80(92:104): cast off 7(7:8)sts, patt to end
*Dec neck edge on next 5 rows. Dec neck edge on alt rows to 19(23:24)sts.
Cont to completion of row 90(104:120).
Cast (bind) off.

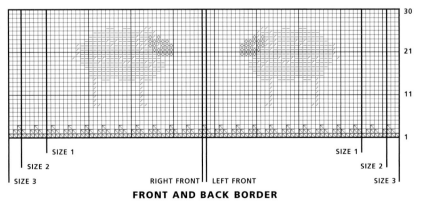

FRONT AND BACK BORDER

- ☐ NAVY (M)
- ◇ YELLOW (A)
- ◪ BLUE (B)
- ◩ DARK PINK (C)
- ─ ECRU (E)

sheep jacket

RIGHT FRONT

Cast on and rows 1–30 as Left Front. Change to stripe patt as on back noting

ROW 31: place pocket, using C ; k6, place next 26sts on holder, knit 26sts from pocket, k5(11:14)

ROW 35: 2B ✳ 1F 3B ✳ to last 3(1:3)sts, 1F 2(0:2)B

ROW 36: ✳1C 1F ✳ to last st, 1C

Armhole

ROW 58(68:78): cast off 4(5:6)sts, patt to end

Neck

ROW 79(91:103): cast off 7(7:8)sts, patt to end. Work ✳ to ✳ as on Left Front Neck

SLEEVES

Using 3¼mm (US 3) needles and M, cast on 37(39:41)sts and work 10 rows in moss stitch. Change to 4mm (US 6) needles and stocking (stockinette) stitch and stripe patt as on back. Inc each end of 3rd and every foll 4th row to 57(61:69)sts, working extra sts into patt. Cont without shaping until work measures 20(25:30)cm (8:10:12in). Place markers at each end of last row. Work further 4(6:6) rows. Cast off.

POCKET TRIMS

Using 3¼mm (US 3) needles and C, knit across 26sts on holder. Work 5 rows in moss stitch. Cast (bind) off loosely in moss stitch.

EDGING

Using 3¼mm (US 3) needles and C, cast on 2sts.

ROW 1: k2.

ROW 2: inc, k1.

ROW 3: k1 p1 inc.

ROW 4: inc, k1 p1 k1.

ROWS 5–8: moss stitch, inc at shaped edge on every row. *(9sts)*

ROW 9: moss stitch.

ROWS 10–16: dec at shaped edge on each row, moss stitch. *(2sts)*

Repeat rows 1–16 until straight edge fits lower edge of garment, ending after a complete patt repeat.

BUTTONBAND

Using 3¼mm (US 3) needles and C, cast on 6sts and work in moss stitch until band, when slightly stretched, fits front to neck shaping. Cast (bind) off. Sew into place. Mark positions for 5 buttons, the first and last 1cm (½in) from top and bottom edges and remaining 3 evenly spaced between.

BUTTONHOLE BAND

Work to match buttonband making buttonholes to match button positions by: moss 2, k2tog, yrn, moss 2.

COLLAR

Join shoulder seams. Using 3¼mm (US 3) needles and C, with right side facing and beginning and ending at centre of front bands, pick up and knit 73(77:81)sts from neck. Work as folls:–

ROWS 1–2: k2, moss to last 2sts, k2.

ROW 3: k2, moss to last 3sts, inc, k2.

Repeat row 3 until collar measures 6cm (2¾in). Cast (bind) off loosely in moss stitch.

MAKING UP

Weave in any loose ends. Slipstitch pockets and pocket trims into position. Join side seams. Join sleeve seams to marker. Set in sleeves (see diagram on page 95). Attach edging, omitting front bands. Sew on buttons.

SIZES	1	2	3
to fit years	1–2	3–4	5–6
actual size chest cm(in)	66(26)	76(30)	81(32)
back length cm(in)	33(13)	38(15)	44(17½)
sleeve seam cm(in)	20(8)	25(10)	30(12)

MATERIALS

Rowan Designer DK Wool 50g balls or Rowan Wool Cotton 50g balls

navy (M)	2	2	2
yellow (A)	1	1	1
blue (B)	1	1	1
dark pink (C)	2	2	2
turquoise (D)	1	1	1
ecru (E)	1	1	1
light pink (F)	1	1	1

5 buttons

1 pair each 3¼mm (US 3) and 4mm (US 6) needles
Stitch holders

animal blanket

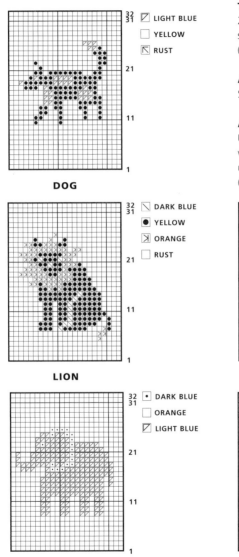

DOG

LIGHT BLUE
YELLOW
RUST

LION

DARK BLUE
YELLOW
ORANGE
RUST

ELEPHANT

DARK BLUE
ORANGE
LIGHT BLUE

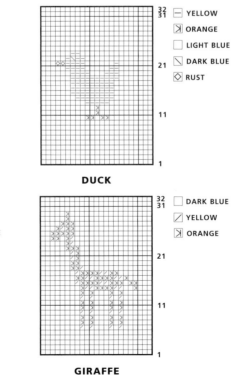

DUCK

YELLOW
ORANGE
LIGHT BLUE
DARK BLUE
RUST

GIRAFFE

DARK BLUE
YELLOW
ORANGE

TENSION (GAUGE)

23sts and 32 rows = 10cm (4in) square over stocking (stockinette) stitch using 3¾mm (US 5) needles.

ABBREVIATIONS

See page 95.

ANIMAL PATCHES

Using background colour, cast on 23sts and working in stocking (stockinette) stitch and using intarsia technique, follow graph. Cast (bind) off.

MOSS STITCH PATCHES

Cast on 23sts. Work 32 rows in moss stitch, [every row: *k1 p1* to last st, k1]. Cast (bind) off in moss stitch.

NUMBER OF PATCHES
Animal patches

dog	4
lion	4
elephant	4
duck	3
giraffe	3

Moss stitch patches

dark blue	3
yellow	4
orange	5
light blue	3
rust	2

Join squares (see diagram opposite).

EDGINGS

Using blue, cast on 2sts, work as folls:– starting with mitre corner.

ROW 1: k2.
ROW 2: inc, k1.
ROW 3: k1 p1, inc.
ROW 4: inc. K1 p1 k1.
ROWS 5–12: moss stitch, inc at shaped edge on every row. *(13sts)*
Cont in moss stitch until shorter edge, when slightly stretched, fits side of blanket. Work 12 more rows, dec 1st per row, making sure that you start dec at the shorter edge, to make mitre corner.
Make three more pieces to fit the other side, top and bottom of blanket.
Attach edgings and join mitre corners. Weave in loose ends.

animal blanket

elephant	light blue	dog	rust	giraffe
yellow	lion	dark blue	duck	orange
giraffe	yellow	elephant	dark blue	dog
orange	duck	yellow	lion	light blue
lion	orange	giraffe	yellow	elephant
light blue	dog	orange	duck	rust
elephant	dark blue	lion	orange	dog

SIZE

width	61cm (24in)
length	81cm (32in)

MATERIALS

Rowan Cotton Glace 50g balls

dark blue	4
yellow	2
orange	2
light blue	2
rust	2

1 pair 3¾mm (US 5) needles

farmyard cushion

TENSION (GAUGE)
20sts and 28 rows = 10cm (4in) square over stocking (stockinette) stitch using 4mm (US 6) needles.

ABBREVIATIONS
See page 95.

FRONT
Using M, cast on 70sts and working in stocking (stockinette) stitch, follow graph. Cast (bind) off.

BACK
Using M, cast on 70sts. Work 50 rows in stocking (stockinette) stitch.
ROWS 51–53: k1 p1 rib.
Buttonhole
ROW 54: *rib 17, cast (bind) off 1st * 3 times, rib 16.
ROW 55: rib 16 *yrn, rib 17 * 3 times.
ROWS 56–58: rib.
Cast (bind) off.
Make 2nd piece omitting buttonholes.

☐	BLUE (M)
⊟	ECRU
▼	GREEN
⊠	RED
◇	YELLOW
◿	NAVY
•	ORANGE
⊡	LIGHT PINK
◢	BLACK
○	BROWN
△	YELLOW CHENILLE

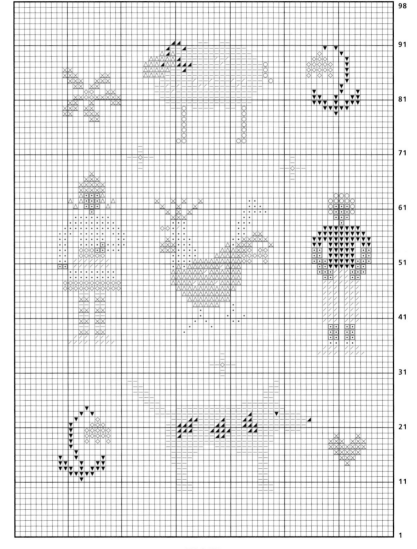

FRONT

farmyard cushion

EDGING

Using colours randomly, but in complete repeats (see photograph), work as folls:–
Cast on 2sts.
ROW 1: k2.
ROW 2: inc, k1.
ROW 3: k1 p1 inc.
ROW 4: inc, k1 p1 k1.
ROWS 5–8: moss stitch, inc at shaped edge on every row. *(9sts)*
ROW 9: moss stitch.
ROWS 10–16: dec at shaped edge on each row, moss stitch. *(2sts)*
Repeat rows 1–16 until there are 34 triangles. Cast (bind) off.

MAKING UP

Weave in any loose ends. Place triangles around cushion, RS together, with points towards cushion centre, pin or tack into place.
Place half backs of cushion over cushion front, RS together, making sure buttonhole back is underneath button back. Sew securely, through all thicknesses, around 4 sides of cushion. Turn RS out. Sew on buttons.

SIZE

36cm (14in) square

MATERIALS

Rowan Handknit DK Cotton 50g balls

blue (M)	4
ecru	1
green	1
red	1
yellow	1
navy	1
orange	1

small amounts of **light pink, black** and **brown**
Rowan Chunky Chenille 50g ball

yellow	1

36cm (14in) square cushion pad
3 buttons

1 pair 4mm (US 6) needles

camel waistcoat

TENSION (GAUGE)
23sts and 32 rows = 10cm (4in) square over stocking (stockinette) stitch using 3¾mm (US 5) needles.

ABBREVIATIONS
See page 95.

BACK
Using 3mm (US 3) needles and M, cast on 65(71:77)sts and work 10 rows in moss stitch, (every row * k1 p1 * to last st, k1). Change to 3¾mm (US 5) needles and stocking (stockinette) stitch. Work rows 1–3 from graph (triangle border), then 3 rows in M. Work in stripe patt of 6 rows each of red, yellow, blue, green and M (30 row repeat) to completion of row 42(54:66).
Shape armhole: (keeping patt correct) cast (bind) off 3(4:3)sts beg next 2 rows.

Size 3
Cast (bind) off 3sts beg next 2 rows.

All sizes
Dec each end of every row to 49(57:57)sts. Dec each end of alt rows to 47(51:53)sts. Cont to completion of row 62(72:90).

Size 2
ROWS 73–76: blue.

All sizes
Place camel: N.B. whilst working camel, omit yellow stripe from patt.
ROW 63 (77:91): patt 15(17:18), knit 17 yellow (1st row of camel graph), patt 15(17:18).
Cont with stripes to completion of camel. Work 4 more rows.
Shape shoulders and neck:
ROW 1: cast (bind) off 6sts, patt 10(12:12)sts, cast (bind) off 15(15:17)sts, patt to end.

ROW 2: cast (bind) off 6sts, patt to end.
ROW 3: cast (bind) off 4(5:5)sts, patt to end.
ROW 4: cast (bind) off.
Rejoin yarn to remaining sts at neck edge and work rows 3–4.

LEFT AND RIGHT FRONTS
Using 3mm (US 3) needles and M, cast on 32(35:38)sts and work 10 rows in moss stitch. Change to 3¾mm (US 5) needles and stocking (stockinette) stitch. Follow graph.

ARMBANDS
Join shoulder seams. Using 3mm (US 3) needles and M, pick up and knit 73(77:85)sts around armhole. Work 5 rows in moss stitch. Cast (bind) off in moss stitch.

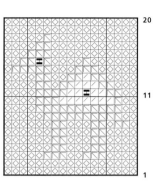

BACK MOTIF

☐ DARK GREY (M)
◩ BLUE
◥ RED
⊟ GREEN
◇ YELLOW

BUTTONBAND
Using 3mm (US 3) needles and M, cast on 6sts and work in moss stitch. Make 4 buttonholes, placing the first 1cm (½in) from cast on, the 4th at start of V–shaping and the other 2 evenly spaced between.
To make buttonhole:
ROW 1: moss 2, cast (bind) off 2sts, moss 2.
ROW 2: moss 2, cast on 2sts, moss 2.
Cont with band until it fits around front edge. Cast (bind) off.

MAKING UP
Join side seams. Attach front band. Sew in any loose ends. Sew on buttons.

camel waistcoat

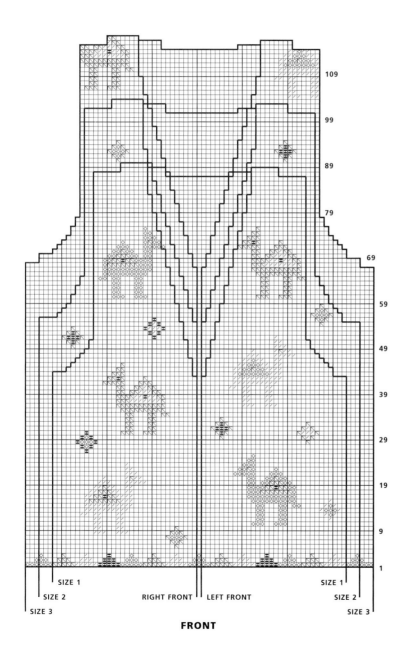

FRONT

SIZE 1
SIZE 2
SIZE 3
RIGHT FRONT   LEFT FRONT
SIZE 1
SIZE 2
SIZE 3

109
99
89
79
69
59
49
39
29
19
9
1

SIZES	1	2	3
to fit years	1–2	3–4	5–6
chest actual cm(in)	56(22)	61(24)	66(26)
back length cm(in)	31(12)	35(14)	40(16)

MATERIALS

Jaegar Merino 50g balls

dark grey (M)	2	2	2
blue	1	1	1
red	1	1	1
green	1	1	1
yellow	1	1	1

4 buttons

1 pair each 3mm (US 3) and 3¾mm (US 5) needles

butterflies and birds jacket

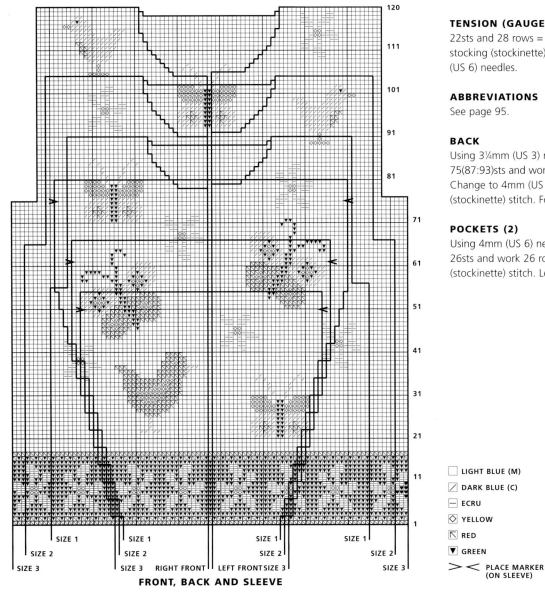

FRONT, BACK AND SLEEVE

TENSION (GAUGE)
22sts and 28 rows = 10cm (4in) square over stocking (stockinette) stitch using 4mm (US 6) needles.

ABBREVIATIONS
See page 95.

BACK
Using 3¼mm (US 3) needles and C, cast on 75(87:93)sts and work 10 rows in moss stitch. Change to 4mm (US 6) needles and stocking (stockinette) stitch. Follow graph.

POCKETS (2)
Using 4mm (US 6) needles and M, cast on 26sts and work 26 rows in stocking (stockinette) stitch. Leave on holder.

☐ LIGHT BLUE (M)
◩ DARK BLUE (C)
⊟ ECRU
◇ YELLOW
◤ RED
▼ GREEN
>< PLACE MARKER (ON SLEEVE)

butterflies and birds jacket

LEFT AND RIGHT FRONTS

Using 3¼mm (US 3) needles and C, cast on 37(43:46)sts and work 10 rows in moss stitch.
Change to 4mm (US 6) needles and stocking (stockinette) stitch. Follow appropriate graph noting;

ROW 31: **Place pocket**

Left Front, k5(11:14), place next 26sts on holder, knit 26sts from pocket, k6.
Right Front, k6, place next 26sts on holder, knit 26sts from pocket, k5(11:14).

SLEEVES

Using 3¼mm (US 3) needles and C, cast on 37(39:41)sts and work 10 rows in moss stitch. Change to 4mm (US 6) needles and stocking (stockinette) stitch. Follow graph.

POCKET TRIMS

Using 3¼mm (US 3) needles and C, knit across 26sts on holder. Work 5 rows in moss stitch. Cast (bind) off loosely in moss stitch.

BUTTONBAND

Using 3¼mm (US 3) needles and C, cast on 6sts and work in moss stitch until band, when slightly stretched, fits front to neck shaping. Cast (bind) off. Sew into place. Mark positions for 5 buttons, the first and last 1cm (½in) from top and bottom edges and remaining 3 evenly spaced between.

BUTTONHOLE BAND

Work to match buttonband making buttonholes to match button positions by: moss 2, k2tog, yrn, moss 2.

COLLAR

Join shoulder seams. Using 3¼mm (US 3) needles and C, with right side facing and beginning and ending at centre of front bands, pick up and knit 73(77:81)sts from neck. Work as folls:–

ROWS 1–2: k2, moss to last 2sts, k2.
ROW 3: k2, moss to last 3sts, inc, k2.
Repeat row 3 until collar measures 6cm (2¾in). Cast (bind) off loosely in moss stitch.

MAKING UP

Weave in any loose ends. Slip stitch pockets and pocket trims into position. Join side seams. Join sleeve seams to marker. Set in sleeves (see diagram on page 95). Sew on buttons.

SIZES

	1	2	3
to fit years	1–2	3–4	5–6
actual size chest cm(in)	66(26)	76(30)	81(32)
back length cm(in)	33(13)	38(15)	44(17½)
sleeve seam cm(in)	20(8)	25(10)	30(12)

MATERIALS

Rowan Designer DK Wool 50g balls or Rowan Wool Cotton 50g balls

light blue (M)	4	5	6
dark blue (C)	2	2	2
ecru	1	1	1
yellow	1	1	1
red	1	1	1
green	1	1	1

5 buttons

1 pair each 3¼mm (US 3) and 4mm (US 6) needles
Stitch holders

butterfly sweater

TENSION (GAUGE)

20sts and 28 rows = 10cm (4in) square over stocking (stockinette) stitch using 4mm (US 6) needles.

ABBREVIATIONS

See page 95.

BACK

Using 3¼mm (US 3) needles and C, cast on 68(76:84)sts and knit 10 rows.
Change to 4mm (US 6) needles and stocking (stockinette) stitch. Work rows 1–17 from border chart. Change to M and cont to completion of row 48(58:72).
Shape armhole: cast (bind) off 4(5:5)sts beg next two rows.
Cont to completion of row 81(95:113).
Shape neck: WS facing, p18(20:23) p2tog turn.
∗ On 19(21:24)sts, dec neck edge on next 2 rows. Cast (bind) off. ∗
Slip 20(22:24)sts on holder. Rejoin yarn to remaining sts at neck edge, p2tog purl to end. Work ∗ to ∗ again.

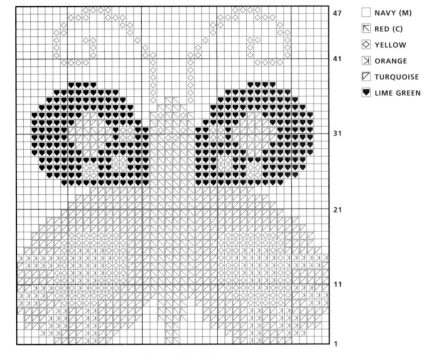

FRONT MOTIF

NAVY (M)
RED (C)
YELLOW
ORANGE
TURQUOISE
LIME GREEN

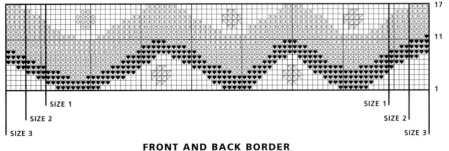

SIZE 1
SIZE 2
SIZE 3
SIZE 1
SIZE 2
SIZE 3

FRONT AND BACK BORDER

butterfly sweater

FRONT

Cast on and welt as back. Change to 4mm (US 6) needles and stocking (stockinette) stitch. Work border chart.
Change to M and cont to completion of row 22(28:40).
Place butterfly: NEXT ROW: 13(17:21)M, 42sts of row 1 of graph, 13(17:21)M.
Complete butterfly from graph, casting (binding) off 4(5:5)sts beg of chart rows 27 and 28(31 and 32: 33 and 34) for armholes. Work further 3(9:13) rows.

Shape neck:
ROW 1: k24(26:30) turn.
✳ **ROWS 2–4:** dec neck edge.
ROWS 5–11 (11:13): dec neck edge on alt rows. *(17:19:22sts)*
Work further 3(5:5) rows.
Cast (bind) off. ✳
Place centre 12(14:14)sts on holder. Rejoin yarn to remaining sts at neck edge and knit to end. Work ✳ to ✳ again.

SLEEVES

Using 3¼mm (US 3) needles and C, cast on 35(37:39)sts and knit 10 rows.
Change to 4mm (US 6) needles and stocking (stockinette) stitch. Work rows 1–17 from border graph, inc each end of rows 3, 7, 11 and 15. Change to M and cont incs on every foll 4th row to 53(59:63)sts. Cont without shaping until work measures 20(25:30)cm (8:10:12in). Place markers at each end of last row. Work further 4(6:6) rows. Cast (bind) off.

NECKBAND

Join right shoulder seam. With RS facing and using 3¼mm (US 3) needles and C, pick up and knit 14(16:18)sts from side front neck, 12(14:14)sts from holder, 14(16:18)sts from side front neck, 3(4:3)sts from side back neck, 20(22:24)sts from holder and 3(4:3)sts from side back neck.
Knit 9 rows. Cast (bind) off loosely.

MAKING UP

Join left shoulder seam and neckband. Join side seams. Join sleeve seams to marker. Set in sleeves (see diagram on page 95) and stitch into place. Weave in any loose ends.

SIZES

SIZES	1	2	3
to fit years	1–2	3–4	5–6
actual size chest cm(in)	66(26)	76(30)	81(32)
back length cm(in)	33(13)	38(15)	44(17½)
sleeve seam cm(in)	20(8)	25(10)	30(12)

MATERIALS

Rowan Handknit DK Cotton 50g balls

navy (M)	4	5	6
red (C)	2	2	2
yellow	1	1	1
orange	1	1	1
turquoise	1	1	1
lime green	1	1	1

1 pair each 3¼mm (US 3) and 4mm (US 6) needles
Stitch holders

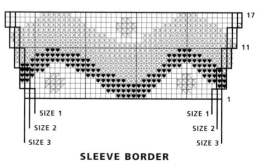

SLEEVE BORDER

- ☐ NAVY (M)
- ◩ RED (C)
- ◇ YELLOW
- ⊠ ORANGE
- ▨ TURQUOISE
- ◆ LIME GREEN

lion rucksack

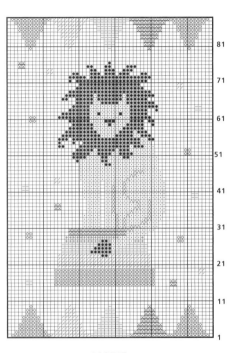

SIZE.

28cm (11in) wide and 34cm (13½in) deep

MATERIALS

Rowan Handknit DK Cotton 50gm balls

navy (M)	4
red	1
blue	1
yellow	1
orange	1
green	1

small amount of **brown** and **black**

Rowan Chunky Chenille 50g ball

gold	1

1 pair 4mm (US 6) needles

TENSION (GAUGE)

20sts and 28 rows = 10cm (4in) square over stocking (stockinette) stitch using 4mm (US 6) needles.

ABBREVIATIONS

See page 95.

BAG

Using red, cast on 57sts and work 12 rows in stocking (stockinette) stitch.

ROW 13: k26, cast (bind) off 1st, k3, cast (bind) off 1st, k26.

ROW 14: p26 yrn p3 yrn p26.

ROWS 15–18: stocking (stockinette) stitch.

Change to M and work 88 rows in stocking (stockinette) stitch.

Work rows 1–88 from graph, using intarsia technique.

Change to red and work 18 rows in stocking (stockinette) stitch. Cast (bind) off.

CORD

Using navy, cast on 6sts and work in stocking (stockinette) stitch for 150cm (59in). Cast (bind) off.

MAKING UP

Weave in any loose ends. Fold bag in half, cast on edge to cast (bound) off edge, and sew side seams. Fold red top in half to the inside and slipstitch into place. Thread cord through holes at top. Stitch ends to side seams at bottom corners of bag making sure that a half knot is made (to loosen and tighten top of bag) and the cord from the left hand hole is sewn to the right hand corner and vice versa.

MOTIF

☐	NAVY (M)
☒	RED
╱	BLUE
◇	YELLOW
•	ORANGE
▬	GREEN
△	BROWN
■	BLACK
⬤	GOLD CHENILLE

e l e p h a n t   b a g

TENSION (GAUGE)
20sts and 28 rows = 10cm (4in) square over stocking (stockinette) stitch using 4mm (US 6) needles.

ABBREVIATIONS
See page 95.

BAG
Using A, cast on 62sts and work as folls:–

ROW 1: ✳k1 p1✳ to end.
ROW 2: ✳p1 k1✳ to end.
ROWS 3–8: as rows 1–2 three times.
ROW 9: as row 1.
Change to stocking (stockinette) stitch.
ROWS 10–18: (starting with a purl row) B.
ROWS 19–26: C.
ROWS 27–34: B.
ROWS 35–42: C.
ROWS 43–50: B.
ROWS 51–58: C.
ROW 59: B.
ROWS 60–68: moss stitch.
ROWS 69–117: using stocking (stockinette) stitch, follow graph.
ROW 118: using A, purl.
ROWS 119–126: moss stitch.
ROW 127: cast (bind) off.

STRAP
Using A, cast on 8sts. Work 132cm (52in) in moss stitch. Cast (bind) off.

MAKING UP
Weave in any loose ends. Fold bag in half. Attach one end of strap to moss stitch section in middle of bag. Sew each side of strap to sides of bag. Repeat for other side making sure strap is NOT twisted (see photograph).

SIZE
32cm (12½in) wide by 20cm (8in) deep

MATERIALS
Rowan Handknit DK Cotton 50g balls

red (A)	2
turquoise (B)	1
lime green (C)	1
small amount of **yellow**	

1 pair 4mm (US 6) needles

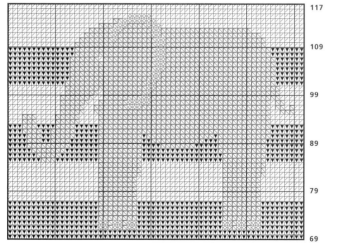

117
109
99
89
79
69

◥ RED (A)
◿ TURQUOISE (B)
▼ LIME GREEN (C)
◇ YELLOW

FRONT MOTIF

elephant jacket

TENSION (GAUGE)

20sts and 28 rows = 10cm (4in) square over stocking (stockinette) stitch using 4mm (US 6) needles.

ABBREVIATIONS

See page 95 and
m1 = pick up yarn before next stitch and knit into the back of made loop.

BACK

Using 3¼mm (US 3) needles and C, cast on 66(74:82)sts and knit 10 rows.
Change to 4mm (US 6) needles and stocking (stockinette) stitch. Follow graph.

LEFT AND RIGHT FRONTS

Using 3¼mm (US 3) needles and C, cast on 33(37:41)sts and knit 10 rows. Change to 4mm (US 6) needles and stocking (stockinette) stitch. Follow graph.

☐ ECRU
◨ RED (C)
◪ ORANGE
◹ BLUE
◇ YELLOW
▼ LIME GREEN
＞＜ PLACE MARKER

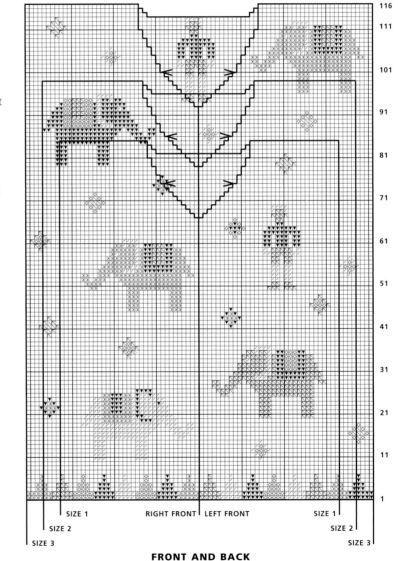

SIZE 1
SIZE 2
SIZE 3
RIGHT FRONT | LEFT FRONT
SIZE 1
SIZE 2
SIZE 3

FRONT AND BACK

elephant jacket

SLEEVES

Using 3¼mm (US 3) needles and C, cast on 33(35:37)sts and knit 10 rows. Change to 4mm (US 6) needles and stocking (stockinette) stitch. Follow graph.

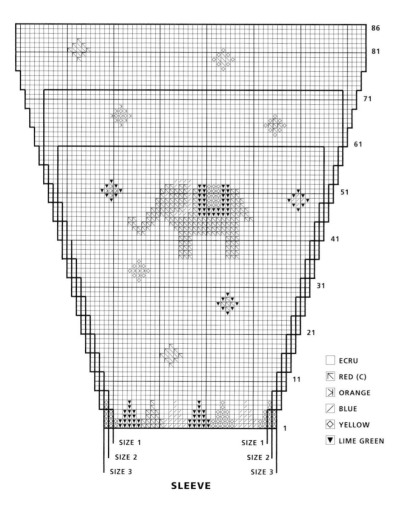

	ECRU
	RED (C)
	ORANGE
	BLUE
	YELLOW
	LIME GREEN

SLEEVE

SIZES	**1**	**2**	**3**
to fit years	1–2	3–4	5–6
actual size chest cm(in)	66(26)	76(30)	81(32)
back length cm(in)	33(13)	38(15)	44(17½)
sleeve seam cm(in)	20(8)	25(10)	30(12)

MATERIALS

Rowan Handknit DK Cotton 50g balls

ecru	4	5	6
red (C)	2	2	2
orange	1	1	1
blue	1	1	1
yellow	1	1	1
lime green	1	1	1

5 buttons

1 pair each 3¼mm (US 3) and 4mm (US 6) needles

69

FRONT BANDS AND COLLAR

Band

Using 3mm (US 3) needles and C, cast on
6sts and knit 4 rows.
❋ROW 5: k3, cast (bind) off 1st, k2.
ROW 6: k2, yrn, k3.
Knit 22(26:30) rows ❋. Repeat ❋ to ❋ 3 more
times. *(100:116:132 rows)*
Work rows 5–6 again.
NEXT ROW: cast (bind) off 3sts, k3.

Collar

ROW 1: k3.
ROW 2: k2, turn.
ROW 3: s1, k1.
ROW 4: k2 m1 k1.
ROW 5: k4.
ROW 6: k3, turn.
ROW 7: s1 k2.
ROW 8: k3 m1 k1.
ROW 9: k5.
ROW 10: k4, turn.
ROW 11: s1 k3.
ROW 12: k4 m1 k1.
ROW 13: k6.
ROW 14: k4, turn, s1 k3.
ROW 15: k4 m1 k1, turn, s1 k5.
ROW 16: k6 m1 k1.
ROW 17: k8.
ROW 18: k7, turn.
ROW 19: s1 k6.
ROW 20: k7 m1 k1.
ROW 21: k9.
ROW 22: k8, turn.
ROW 23: s1 k7.
ROW 24: k8 m1 k1.
ROW 25: k10.
ROW 26: k8, turn s1 k7.
ROW 27: k8 m1 k1, turn, s1 k9.
ROW 28: k10 m1 k1.

ROW 29: k12, place marker beg row.
Cont as folls:–
❋ROW 1: k10, turn.
ROW 2: s1 k9.
ROWS 3–6: k12. ❋
Repeat rows 1–6 until shorter edge from
collar marker fits from marker on right front
neck, round back neck to marker on left
front neck, place marker at shorter edge.
Cont as folls:–
ROW 1: k8 k2tog, turn, s1 k8.
ROW 2: k8 k2tog, turn, s1 k8.
ROWS 3–4: k10.
ROW 5: k7 k2tog, turn.
ROW 6: s1 k7.
ROWS 7–8: k9.
ROW 9: k6 k2tog, turn.
ROW 10: s1 k6.

ROWS 11–12: k8.
ROWS 13–14: k4 k2tog, turn, s1 k4.
ROWS 15–16: k6.
ROW 17: k3 k2tog, turn.
ROW 18: s1 k3.
ROWS 19–20: k5.
ROW 21: k2 k2tog, turn.
ROW 22: s1 k2.
ROWS 23–24: k4.
ROW 25: k1 k2tog, turn.
ROW 26: s1 k1.
ROW 27: k3.
ROW 28: k3, cast on 3sts.
Knit further 102(118:134) rows.
Cast (bind) off.

MAKING UP

Measure 14(15:16)cm (5½:6:6¼in) down
from shoulder seams, place pins. Set
sleevehead between pins and stitch. Join
sleeve and side seams. Weave in any loose
ends. Attach bands and collar, matching
markers. Sew on buttons.

tiger-stripe jacket

TENSION (GAUGE)
22sts and 28 rows = 10cm (4in) square over stocking (stockinette) stitch using 4mm (US 6) needles.

ABBREVIATIONS
See page 95.

BACK
Using 3¼mm (US 3) needles and C, cast on 75(87:93)sts and work 10 rows in moss stitch. Change to 4mm (US 6) needles and stocking (stockinette) stitch. Follow graph.

POCKETS (2)
Using 4mm (US 6) needles and M, cast on 26sts and work 26 rows in stocking (stockinette) stitch. Leave on holder.

LEFT AND RIGHT FRONTS
Using 3¼mm (US 3) needles and C, cast on 37(43:46)sts and work 10 rows in moss stitch.
Change to 4mm (US 6) needles and stocking (stockinette) stitch. Follow appropriate graph noting;
ROW 31: Place pocket
Left Front, k5(11:14), place next 26sts on holder, knit 26sts from pocket, k6.
Right Front, k6, place next 26sts on holder, knit 26sts from pocket, k5(11:14).

SLEEVES
Using 3¼mm (US 3) needles and C, cast on 37(39:41)sts and work 10 rows in moss stitch. Change to 4mm (US 6) needles and stocking (stockinette) stitch. Follow graph.

POCKET TRIMS
Using 3¼mm (US 3) needles and C, knit across 26sts on holder. Work 5 rows in moss stitch. Cast (bind) off loosely in moss stitch.

BUTTONBAND
Using 3¼mm (US 3) needles and C, cast on 6sts and work in moss stitch until band, when slightly stretched, fits front to neck shaping. Cast (bind) off. Sew into place. Mark positions for 5 buttons, the first and last 1cm (½in) from top and bottom edges and remaining 3 evenly spaced between.

BUTTONHOLE BAND
Work to match buttonband making buttonholes to match button positions by: moss 2, k2tog, yrn, moss 2.

SIZES	1	2	3
to fit years	1–2	3–4	5–6
actual size chest cm(in)	66(26)	76(30)	81(32)
back length cm(in)	33(13)	38(15)	44(17½)
sleeve seam cm(in)	20(8)	25(10)	30(12)

MATERIALS
Rowan Designer DK Wool 50g balls or Rowan Wool Cotton 50g balls

sand (M)	3	3	4
black (C)	3	4	4

5 buttons

1 pair each 3¼mm (US 3) and 4mm (US 6) needles
Stitch holders

tiger-stripe jacket

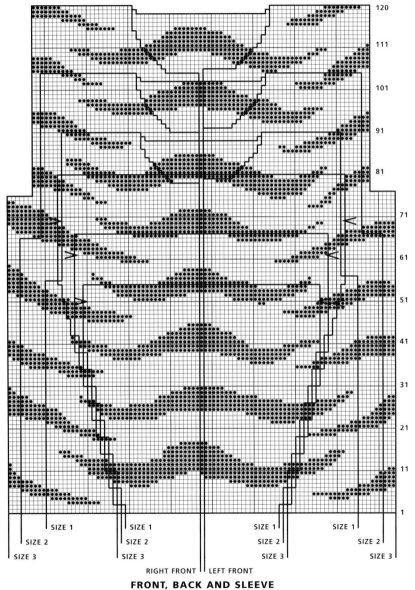

120
111
101
91
81
71
61
51
41
31
21
11
1

SIZE 1   SIZE 1   SIZE 1   SIZE 1
SIZE 2   SIZE 2   SIZE 2   SIZE 2
SIZE 3   SIZE 3   SIZE 3   SIZE 3

RIGHT FRONT | LEFT FRONT

FRONT, BACK AND SLEEVE

☐ SAND (M)

⬤ BLACK (C)

> < PLACE MARKER
(ON SLEEVES)

COLLAR

Join shoulder seams. Using 3¼mm (US 3) needles and C, with right side facing and beginning and ending at centre of front bands, pick up and knit 73(77:81)sts from neck. Work as folls:–

ROWS 1–2: k2, moss to last 2sts, k2.

ROW 3: k2, moss to last 3sts, inc, k2.

Repeat row 3 until collar measures 6cm (2¾in). Cast (bind) off loosely in moss stitch.

MAKING UP

Weave in any loose ends. Slipstitch pockets and pocket trims into position. Join side seams. Join sleeve seams to marker. Set in sleeves (see diagram on page 95). Sew on buttons.

farm sweater

TENSION (GAUGE)
20sts and 28 rows = 10cm (4in) square over stocking (stockinette) stitch using 4mm (US 6) needles.

ABBREVIATIONS
See page 95.

BACK AND FRONT
Using 4mm (US 6) needles and M, cast on 65(80:85)sts. Working in stocking (stockinette) stitch, follow graph leaving centre neck sts on holders.

SLEEVES
Using 3¼mm (US 3) needles and C, cast on 36(38:40)sts and knit 10 rows. Change to 4mm (US 6) needles and stocking (stockinette) stitch and follow graph.

NECKBAND
Join right shoulder seam. With RS facing and using 3¼mm (US 3) needles and C, pick up and knit 14(16:18)sts from side front neck, 11(12:13)sts from holder, 14(16:18)sts from side front neck, 3sts from side back neck, 23(24:25)sts from holder and 3sts from side back neck.
Knit 9 rows. Cast (bind) off loosely.

EDGING
Using 3¼mm (US 3) needles and C, cast on 2sts, work as folls:–
Cast on 2sts.
ROW 1: k2.
ROW 2: inc, k1.
ROW 3: k1 p1 inc.
ROW 4: inc, k1 p1 k1.
ROWS 5–8: moss stitch, inc at shaped edge on every row. *(9sts)*
ROW 9: moss stitch.
ROWS 10–16: dec at shaped edge on each row, moss stitch. *(2sts)*
Repeat rows 1–16 and continue until edging fits lower edge of sweater. Cast (bind) off.

SIZES

	1	2	3
to fit years	1–2	3–4	5–6
actual size chest cm(in)	66(26)	79(31)	84(33)
back length cm(in) (excluding edging)	33(13)	38(15)	44(17½)
sleeve seam cm(in)	21(8½)	25(10)	30(12)

MATERIALS
Rowan Handknit DK Cotton 50g balls

dark blue (M)	4	5	6
red (C)	2	2	2
yellow	1	1	1
green	1	1	1
orange	1	1	1
light blue	1	1	1
ecru	1	1	1

small amount of **brown** and **skin pink**

1 pair each 3¼mm (US 3) and 4mm (US 6) needles
Stitch holders

farm sweater

MAKING UP

Join left shoulder seam and neckband.
Measure down 14(15:16)cm (5½:6:6¼in)
from shoulders, place pins. Set sleeve
head between pins and stitch into position. Join
side and sleeve seams. Attach edging. Weave
in any loose ends.

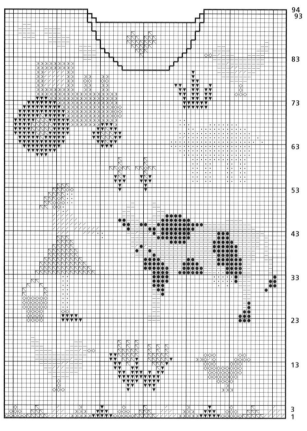

SIZE 1 FRONT AND BACK

☐ DARK BLUE (M)		◹ LIGHT BLUE
◥ RED (C)		⊟ ECRU
◇ YELLOW		● BROWN
▼ GREEN		· SKIN PINK
◪ ORANGE		

farm sweater

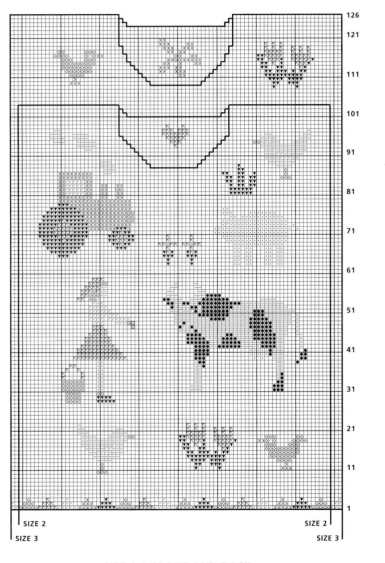

SIZE 2,3 FRONT AND BACK

SIZE 2
SIZE 3
SIZE 2
SIZE 3

126
121
111
101
91
81
71
61
51
41
31
21
11
1

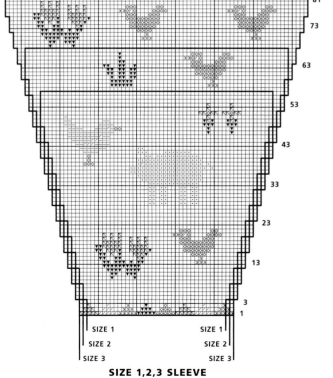

SIZE 1,2,3 SLEEVE

SIZE 1
SIZE 2
SIZE 3
SIZE 1
SIZE 2
SIZE 3

81
73
63
53
43
33
23
13
3
1

toy rabbit

TENSION (GAUGE)
28sts and 38 rows = 10cm (4in) square over stocking (stockinette) stitch using 3mm (US 3) needles.

ABBREVIATIONS
See page 95 and
m1 = pick up yarn before next st and knit into the back of made loop.

SHOES (2)
Start at sole
Using dark pink, cast on 20sts. Work as folls:–
ROW 1: (WS) purl.
ROW 2: * k1 inc * to end. (30sts)
ROW 3: purl.
ROW 4: inc, k11, inc in next 5sts, k11, inc, k1. (37sts)
ROWS 5–9: stocking (stockinette) stitch.
ROW 10: k1 * k2tog k1 * 4 times, * s1 k2tog psso * 4 times, * k1 k2tog * 4 times.
Cast (bind) off knitwise. ** Join heel and sole seams. Turn RS out.
Make second shoe to match.

LEGS (2)
Using ecru cast on 10sts. Work as folls:–
ROW 1: Inc every stitch. (20sts)
ROWS 2–4: stocking (stockinette) stitch.
ROW 5: purl (to mark join with shoe).**
ROWS 6–30: stocking (stockinette) stitch (starting with a purl row).
Break yarn and leave sts on spare needle.
Make second leg to match but DO NOT break yarn.

BODY
ROW 1: knit across both legs. (40sts)
ROWS 2–30: stocking (stockinette) stitch.
ROW 31: k7 * k2tog * 3 times, k14 * k2tog * 3 times, k7.
ROW 32: p1 * p2tog p1 * to end. (23sts)
ROWS 33–36: stocking (stockinette) stitch.
Start head
ROW 37: * k1 m1 * twice, k9 m1 k1 m1 k9 * m1 k1* twice.
Row 38: purl.
ROW 39: k13 * m1 k1 * 3 times, m1 k13. (33sts)
ROWS 40–46: stocking (stockinette) stitch.
ROW 47: k14 k2tog k1 s1 k1 psso k14.
ROW 48: p13 p2togb p1 p2tog p13.
ROW 49: k12 k2tog k1 s1 k1 psso k12.
ROW 50: p11 p2togb p1 p2tog p11.
ROW 51: k5 k2tog k11 k2tog k5. (23sts)
ROWS 52–54: stocking (stockinette) stitch.
ROW 55: * k2tog k2 * twice, k2tog k3 * k2tog k2 * twice, k2tog.
ROW 56: purl.
ROW 57: k1 * k2tog * to end.
ROW 58: p1 * p2tog * to end.
ROW 59: cast (bind) off.

EARS (2)
Using ecru, cast on 8sts. Work as folls:–
ROW 1: (WS) purl.
ROW 2: * k1 m1 k2 m1 k1* twice.
ROW 3: purl.
ROWS 4–5: stocking (stockinette) stitch.
ROW 6: * k2 m1* twice, k4 * m1 k2* twice. (16sts)
ROWS 7–17: stocking (stockinette) stitch.
ROW 18: k2 k2tog s1 k1 psso k4 k2tog s1 k1 psso k2.
ROW 19: purl.

ROW 20: k1 k2tog s1 k1 psso k2 k2tog s1 k1 psso k1.
ROW 21: * p2togb p2tog * twice.
ROW 22: cast (bind) off.
Join centre back seam. Turn RS out.
Make second ear to match.

ARMS (2)
Start with hand
Using ecru, cast on 6sts. Work as folls:–
ROW 1: inc in every stitch.
ROW 2: purl.
ROW 3: knit, inc each end. (14sts)
ROWS 4–6: stocking (stockinette) stitch.
Break ecru, work as folls:–
ROWS 1–4: knit, dark pink.
ROWS 5–8: knit, light pink.
ROWS 9–16: as rows 1–8.
ROWS 17–20: as rows 1–4.
ROW 21: cast (bind) off.
Fold in half lengthwise, RS facing, and join arm and hand seam.
Make second arm to match.

DRESS
Using dark pink, cast on 51sts and work 44 rows in stripe patt as on sleeves.
Keeping stripes correct, work as folls:–
ROW 45: knit.
ROW 46: k9 * k2tog * 3 times, k21, * k2tog * 3 times, k9.
ROW 47: * k1 k2tog * to end. (30sts)
ROWS 48–51: patt.
ROW 52: cast (bind) off.
Join row edge seam.

BOWS (2)
Using dark pink, cast on 5sts. Knit 14 rows.
Cast (bind) off.

t o y   r a b b i t

MAKING UP

Join leg seams. Join centre back seam to
waist level. Join head and centre back seams
to mid chest leaving a small opening for
stuffing. Stuff body firmly and close opening.
Stuff shoes and attach to ends of leg. Sew
firmly joining the two sets of loops formed
on rows ✱✱. Attach dress at neck level. Stuff
arms and pin in desired positions, sew firmly
to body through dress. Attach ears to
shaping lines at either side of head. Wind a
piece of dark pink yarn around centre of bow
and fix to shoes. Embroider facial features
(see photograph).

SIZE

25cm (10in) head to toe

MATERIALS

Rowan Wool Cotton 50g ball

ecru	1
dark pink	1

small amounts of **light pink** and **brown**
Washable toy filling

1 pair 3mm (US 3) needles
Spare needle

toy dog

SIZE
20cm (8in) nose to tail

MATERIALS
Rowan Designer DK Wool 50g ball
ecru   1
small amount of **black**
Washable toy filling

1 pair 3mm (US 3) needles

TENSION (GAUGE)
28sts and 38 rows = 10cm (4in) square over stocking (stockinette) stitch using 3mm (US 3) needles.

ABBREVIATIONS
See page 95.

N.B. Work in stocking (stockinette) stitch throughout, using intarsia technique to knit black markings as you wish. Shaping rows ONLY given.

MAIN PART
Start at back legs: using ecru, cast on 48sts, mark sts 17 and 32.
ROWS 11–12: cast (bind) off 12sts, work to end.
ROWS 21–22: cast on 12sts, work to end.
ROWS 41–42: cast (bind) off 12sts, work to end.
ROW 43: k2tog each end.
ROW 47: k2tog each end.
ROW 51: k2tog k6 s1 k1 psso k2tog k6 k2tog.
ROW 52: p7 p2tog p7.
ROW 55: k2tog each end.
ROW 59: k2tog each end.
ROW 61: cast (bind) off.

GUSSET
Start nose end: using ecru, cast on 2sts.
ROW 3: inc k1.
ROW 9: inc each end.
ROWS 15 AND 19: inc each end. *(9sts)*
ROWS 21–22: cast on 12sts, work to end.
ROWS 31–32: cast (bind) off 12sts, work to end.
ROWS 51–52: cast on 12sts, work to end.
ROW 61: cast (bind) off.

TAIL
Using ecru, cast on 10sts. Work 2 rows in stocking (stockinette) stitch. Cast (bind) off. Join cast (bound) off edge to cast on edge.

EARS (2)
Using ecru, cast on 8sts. Work 2 rows in stocking (stockinette) stitch.
ROW 3: * k1 inc, inc k1* twice.
ROW 11: * k1 s1 k1 psso k2tog k1* twice.
ROW 12: * p1tog p2togb * twice.
ROW 13: cast (bind) off.
Fold in half and join row ends.

MAKING UP
Fold main part in half longwise, RS together, and join cast (bound) off edge (nose). Attach tail to back legs at fold line and stitch backlegs from fold to marked sts. Place gusset to main part, nose point to nose join, legs to legs. Stitch around gusset, leaving a small opening in the stomach area for stuffing. Stuff firmly and close opening. Sew ears to head and embroider facial features (see photograph).

duck jacket

TENSION (GAUGE)

20sts and 28 rows = 10cm (4in) square over stocking (stockinette) stitch using 4mm (US 6) needles.

ABBREVIATIONS

See page 95 and
m1 = pick up yarn before next st and knit into the back of made loop.

BACK

Using 4mm (US 6) needles and M, cast on 61(65:71)sts. Working in stocking (stockinette) stitch, follow graph, (12 rows). Work further 59(67:77) rows, placing daisies randomly (but at least 6sts and 10 rows apart).
Shape neck: WS facing, patt 22(23:24), cast (bind) off 17(19:23)sts, patt 22(23:24).
On 22(23:24)sts, dec neck edge on next 2 rows. Cast (bind) off.
Rejoin yarn to remaining sts and work to match.

RIGHT AND LEFT FRONTS

Using 4mm (US 6) needles and M, cast on 30(32:35)sts. Working in stocking (stockinette) stitch, follow graph. Work further 46(52:60) rows, placing daisies randomly. Dec neck edge on next 8 rows. Place marker at neck edge on row 8. Dec neck edge on alt rows to 20(21:22)sts. Work 4(4:2) more rows. Cast (bind) off.

SLEEVES

Using 3¼mm (US 3) needles and M, cast on 33(35:37)sts and knit 10 rows.
Change to 4mm (US 6) needles and stocking (stockinette) stitch. Placing daisies randomly, inc each end of 5th and every foll 4th rows to 53(57:63)sts. Cont without shaping until work measures 18(20:25)cm (7:8:10in). Cast (bind) off.

SIZES

SIZES		1	2	3
to fit years		6mths–1	1–2	2–3
chest actual cm(in)		61(24)	66(26)	71(28)
back length cm(in)		29(11½)	32(12½)	36(14)
sleeve seam cm(in)		18(7)	20(8)	25(10)

MATERIALS

Rowan Handknit DK Cotton 50g balls

	1	2	3
blue (M)	5	5	6
ecru	1	1	1
yellow	1	1	1

small amount of **orange**
5 buttons

1 pair 3¼mm (US 3) and 4mm (US 6) needles

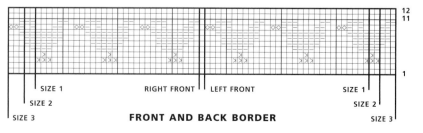

	SIZE 1	RIGHT FRONT	LEFT FRONT	SIZE 1	
	SIZE 2			SIZE 2	
SIZE 3		**FRONT AND BACK BORDER**			SIZE 3

DAISY MOTIF

☐ BLUE (M)
⊟ ECRU
◇ YELLOW
⋈ ORANGE

duck jacket

FRONT BANDS AND COLLAR
Band
Using 3¼mm (US 3) needles and M cast on 6sts and knit 4 rows.
* ROW 5: k3, cast (bind) off 1st, k2.
ROW 6: k2, yrn, k3.
Knit 20(22:24) rows *. Repeat * to * 3 more times. *(92:100:108 rows)*
Work rows 5–6 again. Next row: cast (bind) off 3sts, k3.

Start Collar
ROW 1: k3.
ROW 2: k2, turn.
ROW 3: s1, k1.
ROW 4: k2 m1 k1.
ROW 5: k4.
ROW 6: k3, turn.
ROW 7: s1 k2.
ROW 8: k3 m1 k1.
ROW 9: k5.
ROW 10: k4, turn.
ROW 11: s1 k3.
ROW 12: k4 m1 k1.
ROW 13: k6.
ROW 14: k4, turn, s1 k3.
ROW 15: k4 m1 k1, turn, s1 k5.
ROW 16: k6 m1 k1.
ROW 17: k8.
ROW 18: k7, turn.
ROW 19: s1 k6.
ROW 20: k7 m1 k1.
ROW 21: k9.
ROW 22: k8, turn.
ROW 23: s1 k7.
ROW 24: k8 m1 k1.
ROW 25: k10.
ROW 26: k8, turn s1 k7.
ROW 27: k8 m1 k1, turn, s1 k9.
ROW 28: k10 m1 k1.

ROW 29: k12, place marker beg row.
Cont as folls:–
* ROW 1: k10, turn.
ROW 2: s1 k9.
ROWS 3–6: k12. *
Repeat rows 1–6 until shorter edge from collar marker fits from marker on right front neck, round back neck to marker on left front neck, place marker at shorter edge.
Cont as folls:–
ROW 1: k8 k2tog, turn, s1 k8.
ROW 2: k8 k2tog, turn, s1 k8.
ROWS 3–4: k10.
ROW 5: k7 k2tog, turn.
ROW 6: s1 k7.
ROWS 7–8: k9.
ROW 9: k6 k2tog, turn.
ROW 10: s1 k6.
ROWS 11–12: k8.
ROWS 13–14: k4 k2tog, turn, s1 k4.
ROWS 15–16: k6.

ROW 17: k3 k2tog, turn.
ROW 18: s1 k3.
ROWS 19–20: k5.
ROW 21: k2 k2tog, turn.
ROW 22: s1 k2.
ROWS 23–24: k4.
ROW 25: k1 k2tog, turn.
ROW 26: s1 k1.
ROW 27: k3.
ROW 28: k3, cast on 3sts.
Knit further 94(100:108) rows. Cast (bind) off.

LACE EDGING
Using 4mm (US 6) needles and M, cast on 3sts. Work as folls:–
ROW 1: s1 k2.
ROW 2: k1 yrn k2.
ROW 3: s1 k3.
ROW 4: k1 yrn k3.
ROW 5: s1 k4.
ROW 6: k1 yrn k4.
ROW 7: s1 k5.
ROW 8: k1 yrn s1 k2tog psso k2.
ROW 9: s1 k4.
ROW 10: k1 yrn s1 k2tog psso k1.
ROW 11: s1 k3.
ROW 12: k1 yrn s1 k2tog psso.
ROWS 1–12 form patt repeat. Cont in patt until work fits around bottom edge of garment, omitting front bands and finishing with Row 12. Cast (bind) off.

MAKING UP
Measure 12(13:14)cm (4¾:5:5½) down from shoulder seam, place pin. Set in sleeves between pins and stitch. Join sleeve and side seams. Weave in any loose ends. Attach bands and collar, matching markers. Attach lace edging to garment. Sew on buttons.

tiger sweater

TENSION (GAUGE)

20sts and 28 rows = 10cm (4in) square over stocking (stockinette) stitch using 4mm (US 6) needles.

ABBREVIATIONS

See page 95.

BACK

Using 3¼mm (US 3) needles and orange, cast on 68(76:84)sts. Change to M and work 10 rows in 2 x 2 rib. (Every row ✳ k2 p2 ✳ to end).

Change to 4mm (US 6) needles and work in stocking (stockinette) stitch as folls:–

Sizes 1 & 3

✳ ROWS 1–2: M.
ROW 3: C.
ROWS 4–8: M. ✳

Size 2

✳ ROWS 1–4: M.
ROW 5: C.
ROWS 6–8: M. ✳
ROWS 1–8 form stripe repeat. Cont to completion of row 48(58:72).

Shape armhole: cast (bind) off 4(5:5)sts beg next two rows.
Keeping patt correct, cont to completion of row 81(95:113).

Shape neck: WS facing, p18(20:23) p2tog turn.
✳ On 19(21:24)sts, dec neck edge on next 2 rows. Cast (bind) off. ✳
Slip 20(22:24)sts on holder. Rejoin yarn to remaining sts at neck edge, p2tog purl to end. Work ✳ to ✳ again.

SIZES	1	2	3
to fit years	1–2	3–4	5–6
actual size chest cm(in)	66(26)	76(30)	81(32)
back length cm(in)	33(13)	38(15)	44(17½)
sleeve seam cm(in)	20(8)	25(10)	30(12)

MATERIALS

Rowan Handknit DK Cotton 50g ball

turquoise (M)	4	5	6
green (C)	2	2	2
orange	1	1	1
small amount of **black**			

1 pair each 3¼mm (US 3) and 4mm (US 6) needles
Stitch holders

tiger sweater

FRONT

As back to completion of row 26(36:50).

Place tiger NEXT ROW: green.

ROW 2: 8(12:16)M, 52 green, 8(12:16)M
Complete tiger graph, casting (binding) off
4(5:5)sts beg of chart rows 23 and 24 and
keeping edge sts in stripe patt
(see photograph).
Work further 11(13:15) rows.

Shape neck:

ROW 1: k24(26:30) turn.

＊ROWS 2–4: dec neck edge.

ROWS 5–11 (11:13): dec neck edge on alt
rows. *(17:19:22sts)*
Work further 3(5:5) rows.
Cast (bind) off. ＊
Place centre 12(14:14)sts on holder. Rejoin
yarn to remaining sts at neck edge and knit
to end. Work ＊ to ＊ again.

SLEEVES

Using 3¼mm (US 3) needles and orange, cast
on 36(40:40)sts. Change to M and work
10 rows in 2 x 2 rib as on back.
Change to 4mm (US 6) needles, stocking
(stockinette) stitch and stripe patt as on back.
Inc each end of 5th and every foll 4th row to
52(58:62)sts. Cont without shaping until
work measures 20(25:30)cm (8:10:12in).
Place markers at each end of last row. Work
further 4(6:6) rows. Cast (bind) off.

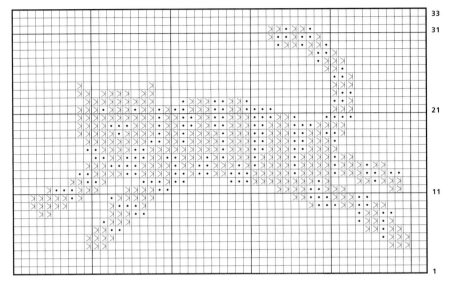

FRONT MOTIF

NECKBAND

Join right shoulder seam. With RS facing and
using 3¼mm (US 3) needles and M, pick up
and knit 14(16:18)sts from side front neck,
12(14:14)sts from holder, 14(16:18)sts from
side front neck, 3(4:3)sts from side back
neck, 20(22:24)sts from holder and 3(4:3)sts
from side back neck.
Work 7 rows in k2 p2 rib.
Change to C and cast (bind) off loosely.

MAKING UP

Join left shoulder seam and neckband. Join
side seams. Join sleeve seams to marker. Set
in sleeves (see diagram on page 95) and
stitch into place. Weave in any loose ends.

☐ GREEN (C)
⊠ ORANGE
• BLACK

fish jacket

TENSION (GAUGE)

20sts and 28 rows = 10cm (4in) square over stocking (stockinette) stitch using 4mm (US 6) needles.

ABBREVIATIONS

See page 95 and
m1 = pick up yarn before next st and knit into the back of made loop.

BACK

Using 3¼mm (US 3) needles and M, cast on 64(74:82)sts and knit 10 rows.
Change to 4mm (US 6) needles and stocking (stockinette) stitch. Work as folls:–
ROWS 1–2: yellow.
ROWS 3–4: turquoise.
ROWS 5–6: lime green.
ROWS 7–8: navy.
ROWS 9–10: orange.
ROWS 11–12: yellow.
ROWS 13–21: follow graph.
Rows 1–21 form patt repeat. Cont in patt until work measures 33(38:46)cm (13:15:18in). Note patt row. ✳✳
Shape neck and shoulders: patt 22(26:28), cast (bind) off 20(22:24)sts, patt 22(26:28). Dec neck edge on next 2 rows.

Cast (bind) off. Rejoin yarn to remaining sts and work to match.

LEFT AND RIGHT FRONTS

Using 3¼mm (US 3) needles and M, cast on 32(37:41)sts and knit 10 rows. Change to 4mm (US 6) needles and stocking (stockinette) stitch. Work in patt as on back until work is 16(18:22) rows less than ✳✳ noted row on back.
Shape neck: dec neck edge on next 8 rows, placing marker at neck edge on row 8. Dec neck edge on alt rows to 20(24:26)sts. Work to match back at shoulder. Cast (bind) off.

SLEEVES

Using 3¼mm (US 3) needles and M, cast on 36(38:40)sts and knit 10 rows. Change to 4mm (US 6) needles, stocking (stockinette) stitch and patt as on back. Inc each end of 3rd and every foll 4(5:6)th rows to 56(60:66)sts, working extra sts into patt. Cont without shaping until work measures 20(25:30)cm (8:10:12in). Cast (bind) off loosely.

SIZES	1	2	3
to fit years	1–2	3–4	5–6
actual size chest cm(in)	66(26)	76(30)	81(32)
back length cm(in)	33(13)	38(15)	44(17½)
sleeve seam cm(in)	20(8)	25(10)	30(12)

MATERIALS

Rowan Handknit DK Cotton 50g balls

navy (M)	2	2	2
turquoise	1	2	2
orange	1	2	2
lime green	1	2	2
yellow	1	2	2

5 buttons

1 pair each 3¼mm (US 3) and 4mm (US 6) needles

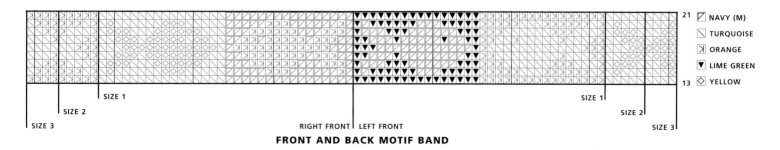

☑	NAVY (M)
◨	TURQUOISE
⊠	ORANGE
▼	LIME GREEN
◇	YELLOW

FRONT AND BACK MOTIF BAND

SIZE 1 SIZE 2 SIZE 3 RIGHT FRONT | LEFT FRONT SIZE 1 SIZE 2 SIZE 3

21

13

fish jacket

FRONT BANDS AND COLLAR
Band
Using 3¼mm (US 3) needles and M, cast on 6sts and knit 4 rows.
✻**ROW 5:** k3, cast (bind) off 1st, k2.
ROW 6: k2, yrn, k3.
Knit 22(26:30) rows ✻. Repeat ✻ to ✻ 3 more times. *(100:116:132 rows)*
Work rows 5–6 again.
NEXT ROW: cast (bind) off 3sts, k3.
Start Collar
ROW 1: k3.
ROW 2: k2, turn.
ROW 3: s1, k1.
ROW 4: k2 m1 k1.
ROW 5: k4.
ROW 6: k3, turn.
ROW 7: s1 k2.
ROW 8: k3 m1 k1.
ROW 9: k5.
ROW 10: k4, turn.
ROW 11: s1 k3.
ROW 12: k4 m1 k1.
ROW 13: k6.
ROW 14: k4, turn, s1 k3.
ROW 15: k4 m1 k1, turn, s1 k5.
ROW 16: k6 m1 k1.
ROW 17: k8.
ROW 18: k7, turn.
ROW 19: s1 k6.
ROW 20: k7 m1 k1.
ROW 21: k9.
ROW 22: k8, turn.
ROW 23: s1 k7.
ROW 24: k8 m1 k1.
ROW 25: k10.
ROW 26: k8, turn s1 k7.
ROW 27: k8 m1 k1, turn, s1 k9.
ROW 28: k10 m1 k1.

ROW 29: k12, place marker beg row.
Cont as folls:–
✻**ROW 1:** k10, turn.
ROW 2: s1 k9.
ROWS 3–6: k12. ✻
Repeat rows 1–6 until shorter edge from collar marker fits from marker on right front neck, round back neck to marker on left front neck, place marker at shorter edge.
Cont as folls:–
ROW 1: k8 k2tog, turn, s1 k8.
ROW 2: k8 k2tog, turn, s1 k8.
ROWS 3–4: k10.
ROW 5: k7 k2tog, turn.
ROW 6: s1 k7.
ROWS 7–8: k9.
ROW 9: k6 k2tog, turn.
ROW 10: s1 k6.
ROWS 11–12: k8.
ROWS 13–14: k4 k2tog, turn, s1 k4.
ROWS 15–16: k6.
ROW 17: k3 k2tog, turn.
ROW 18: s1 k3.
ROWS 19–20: k5.
ROW 21: k2 k2tog, turn.
ROW 22: s1 k2.
ROWS 23–24: k4.
ROW 25: k1 k2tog, turn.
ROW 26: s1 k1.
ROW 27: k3.
ROW 28: k3, cast on 3sts.
Knit further 102(118:134) rows.
Cast (bind) off.

MAKING UP
Measure 14(15:16)cm (5½:6:6¼in) down from shoulder seams, place pins. Set sleevehead between pins and stitch. Join sleeve and side seams. Weave in any loose ends. Attach bands and collar, matching markers. Sew on buttons.

fish hat

TENSION (GAUGE)

20sts and 28 rows = 10cm (4in) square over stocking (stockinette) stitch using 4mm (US 6) needles.

ABBREVIATIONS

See page 95.

EAR FLAPS (MAKE 2)

Using 4mm (US 6) needles and yellow, cast on 7(9:11)sts and work in stocking (stockinette) stitch as folls:–

ROWS 1–2: inc each end.
ROW 3: turquoise.
ROW 4: turquoise, inc each end.
ROW 5: lime green, inc each end.
ROW 6: lime green.
ROW 7: navy, inc each end. *(17:19:21sts)*
ROW 8: navy.
ROWS 9–10: orange.
ROWS 11–12: yellow.
ROW 13–14: turquoise.
ROW 15: lime green.
Size 1; leave sts on spare needle.
Size 2: ROW 16: lime green.
ROW 17: orange, leave sts on spare needle.
Size 3: ROW 16: lime green.
ROWS 17–18: orange.
ROW 19: navy, leave sts on spare needle.

MAIN PART

Using 3¾mm (US 5) needles and navy, cast on 12(14:17)sts, purl across ear flap, cast on 32(36:44)sts, purl across ear flap, cast on 12(14:17)sts. *(90:102:120sts)*
Work as folls:–
ROW 1: RS facing, using navy, purl.
ROWS 2–3: using turquoise, purl.
ROW 4: using yellow, purl.
Change to 4mm (US 6) needles and stocking (stockinette) stitch. Work rows 1–9 from graph.
ROW 10: yellow.

SIZES	1	2	3
to fit years	1–2	3–4	5–6

MATERIALS

Rowan Handknit DK Cotton 50g balls

	1	2	3
navy	1	1	1
turquoise	1	1	1
orange	1	1	1
lime green	1	1	1
yellow	1	1	1

1 pair each 3¾mm (US 5) and 4mm (US 6) needles
Spare needle

- ☑ NAVY
- ◨ TURQUOISE
- ◩ ORANGE
- ▼ LIME GREEN
- ◇ YELLOW

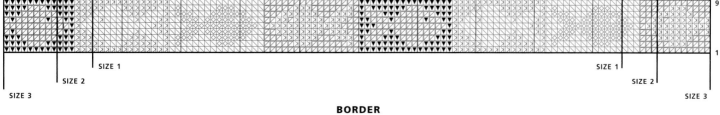

SIZE 1
SIZE 2
SIZE 3
SIZE 1
SIZE 2
SIZE 3

BORDER

f i s h   h a t

Working in 2 row stripes of turquoise, lime green, navy, orange and yellow, (10 row repeat), cont as folls:–

Size 1: work 6 rows. Size 2: work 8 rows, dec each end of row 8. Size 3: work 10 rows. *(90:100:120sts)*

Shape top (all sizes) keep stripe patt correct. Dec rows only given.

ROW 2: * p2tog p8 * to end.

ROW 5: * k7 k2tog * to end.

ROW 8: * p2tog p6 to end.

ROW 11: * k5 k2tog * to end. *(54:60:72sts)*

Size 1:

ROW 12: * p2tog p4 * to end.

ROW 13: * k3 k2tog * to end.

ROW 14: * p2tog * to end.

ROW 15: * k2tog * to end.

Size 2:

ROW 13: * k4 k2tog * to end.

ROW 15: * k3 k2tog * to end. *(40sts)*

ROW 16: * p2tog * to end.

ROW 17: * k2tog * to end.

Size 3:

ROWS 13–15: as Size 2.

ROW 17: * k2 k2tog * to end.

ROW 18: * p2tog p1 * to end.

ROW 19: * k2tog * to end.

All Sizes:

Thread yarn through remaining sts, draw tightly and fasten off securely.

EDGING

With RS facing and using 3¾mm (US 5) needles and navy, pick up and knit 12(14:17)sts from back cast on edge, 31(37:43)sts around ear flap, 32(36:44)sts from front cast on edge, 31(37:43)sts around ear flap and 12(14:17)sts from back cast on edge. Cast (bind) off knitwise.

MAKING UP

Join back seam. Weave in any loose ends. Cut three 60cm (24in) lengths of navy. Thread half the length through bottom centre of ear flap. Taking one end from front and one end from back, make a plait with two ends per strand. Knot at end and trim. Repeat for second earflap.

cow-print scarf
and hat

Scarf

TENSION (GAUGE)
22sts and 28 rows = 10cm (4in) square over stocking (stockinette) stitch using 4mm (US 6) needles.

ABBREVIATIONS
See page 95.

SCARF
Wind off small amounts of yarn and use instarsia technique. Using C, cast on 47sts and work rows 1–36 from graph. Cont repeating rows 7–36 until work measures 108cm (42in), ending with a WS row.
NEXT ROW: Using C, moss 5, k37, moss 5. Work 5 rows in moss stitch. Cast (bind) off in moss stitch. Weave in any loose ends.

Hat

TENSION
23sts and 30 rows = 10cm (4in) square over stocking (stockinette) stitch using 3¾mm (US 5) needles.

HAT
Using 3¼mm (US 3) needles and C, cast on 47(53:57)sts and work 18(20:20) rows in moss stitch, (every row ✳ k1 p1✳ to last st, k1). Change to 3¾mm (US 5) needles and stocking (stockinette) stitch. Work rows 1–36, repeating graph, until work measures 26(30:34)cm (10:12:13½in), ending with a WS row.
NEXT ROW: using 3¼mm (US 3) needles and C, knit. Work 17(19:19) rows in moss stitch. Cast (bind) off in moss stitch.

MAKING UP
Weave in any loose ends. Fold hat in half, cast on edge to cast (bound) off edge, and join side seams. Make two tassels and attach one to each top corner of hat.

Scarf

SIZE
21cm (8½in) by 110cm (43in)

MATERIALS
Rowan Designer DK Wool 50g balls or Rowan Wool Cotton 50g balls

ecru (M)	2
black (C)	2

1 pair 4mm (US 6) needles

Hat

SIZES

	1	**2**	**3**
to fit years	1–2	3–4	5–6

MATERIALS
Rowan Designer DK Wool 50g balls

ecru (M)	1	1	1
black (C)	1	1	1

1 pair each 3¼mm (US 3) and 3¾mm (US 5) needles

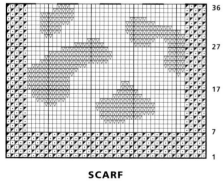

SCARF

- ⚫ C, KNIT ON RS, PURL ON WS
- ◼ C, PURL ON RS, KNIT ON WS } MOSS STITCH
- ☐ ECRU (M), STOCKING (STOCKINETTE) STITCH
- ▽ BLACK (C), STOCKING (STOCKINETTE) STITCH

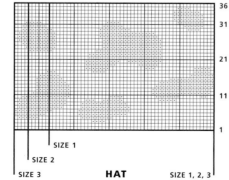

SIZE 1
SIZE 2
SIZE 3   **HAT**   SIZE 1, 2, 3

- ☐ ECRU (M)
- ⚫ BLACK (C)

c o w - p r i n t   j a c k e t

TENSION (GAUGE)
22sts and 28 rows = 10cm (4in) square over stocking (stockinette) stitch using 4mm (US 6) needles.

ABBREVIATIONS
See page 95.

BACK
Using 3¼mm (US 3) needles and C, cast on 75(87:93)sts and work 10 rows in moss stitch. Change to 4mm (US 6) needles and stocking (stockinette) stitch. Follow graph.

POCKETS (2)
Using 4mm (US 6) needles and M, cast on 26sts and work 26 rows in stocking (stockinette) stitch.
Leave on holder.

LEFT AND RIGHT FRONTS
Using 3¼mm (US 3) needles and C, cast on 37(43:46)sts and work 10 rows in moss stitch. Change to 4mm (US 6) needles and stocking (stockinette) stitch. Follow appropriate graph noting;
ROW 31: Place pocket:
Left front, k5(11:14), place next 26sts on holder, knit 26sts from pocket, k6.
Right front, k6, place next 26sts on holder, knit 26sts from pocket, k5(11:14).

SLEEVES
Using 3¼mm (US 3) needles and C, cast on 37(39:41)sts and work 10 rows in moss stitch. Change to 4mm (US 6) needles and stocking (stockinette) stitch. Follow graph.

POCKET TRIMS
Using 3¼mm (US 3) needles and C, knit across 26sts on holder. Work 5 rows in moss stitch. Cast (bind) off loosely in moss stitch.

BUTTONBAND
Using 3¼mm (US 3) needles and C, cast on 6sts and work in moss stitch until band, when slightly stretched, fits front to neck shaping. Cast (bind) off. Sew into place. Mark positions for 5 buttons, the first and last 1cm (½in) from top and bottom edges and remaining 3 evenly spaced between.

BUTTONHOLE BAND
Work to match buttonband making buttonholes to match button positions by: moss 2, k2tog, yrn, moss 2.

COLLAR
Join shoulder seams. Using 3¼mm (US 3) needles and C, with right side facing and beginning and ending at centre of front bands, pick up and knit 73(77:81)sts from neck. Work as folls:–
ROWS 1–2: k2, moss to last 2sts, k2.
ROW 3: k2, moss to last 3sts, inc, k2.
Repeat row 3 until collar measures 6cm (2¾in). Cast (bind) off loosely in moss stitch.

MAKING UP
Weave in any loose ends. Slipstitch pockets and pocket trims into position. Join side seams. Join sleeve seams to marker. Set in sleeves (see diagram on page 95). Sew on buttons.

cow-print jacket

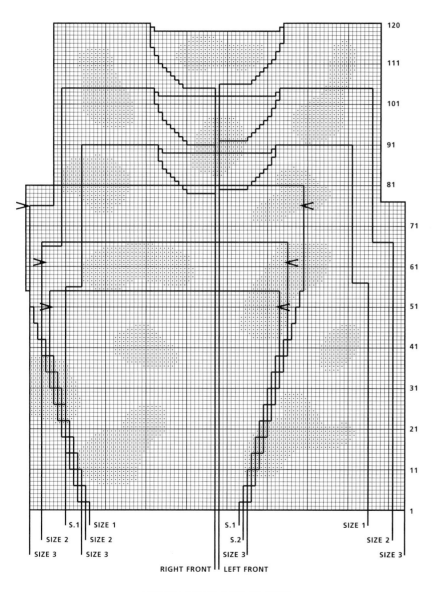

FRONT, BACK AND SLEEVE

RIGHT FRONT | LEFT FRONT

SIZES		**1**	**2**	**3**
	to fit years	1–2	3–4	5–6
	actual size chest cm(in)	66(26)	76(30)	81(32)
	back length cm(in)	33(13)	38(15)	44(17½)
	sleeve seam cm(in)	20(8)	25(10)	30(12)

MATERIALS

Rowan Designer DK Wool 50g balls or Rowan Wool
Cotton 50g balls

ecru (M)	3	3	4
black (C)	3	4	4

5 buttons

1 pair each 3¼mm (US 3) and 4mm (US 6) needles
Stitch holders

☐ ECRU (M)

▪ BLACK (C)

✄ PLACE MARKER
(ON SLEEVES)

r o o s t e r   s w e a t e r

TENSION (GAUGE)

20sts and 28 rows = 10cm (4in) square over stocking (stockinette) stitch using 4mm (US 6) needles.

ABBREVIATIONS

See page 95.

BACK

Using 3¼mm (US 3) needles and C, cast on 68(76:84)sts and work 8 rows in stocking (stockinette) stitch.

ROW 9: change to M and knit.

ROW 10–14: using M, * k2 p2 * to end.
Change to 4mm (US 6) needles and stocking (stockinette) stitch. Work rows 1–15 from border chart. Change to M and cont to completion of row 48(58:72).

Shape armhole: cast (bind) off 4(5:5)sts beg next two rows.
Cont to completion of row 81(95:113).

Shape neck: WS facing, p18(20:23) p2tog turn.
* On 19(21:24)sts, dec neck edge on next 2 rows. Cast (bind) off.*
Slip 20(22:24)sts on holder. Rejoin yarn to remaining sts at neck edge, p2tog purl to end. Work * to * again.

FRONT

Cast on and welt as back. Change to 4mm (US 6) needles and stocking (stockinette) stitch. Work border chart.
Change to M and cont to completion of row 30(40:54).

Place rooster: k31(35:39)M, 3 orange, 4M, 3 orange, 27(31:35)M.
Complete rooster from graph, casting (binding) off 4(5:5)sts beg of chart rows 19 and 20 for armholes.
Work further 7(9:11) rows.

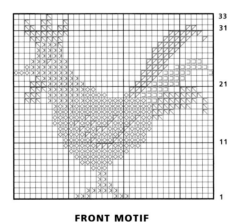

FRONT MOTIF

Shape neck:

ROW 1: k24(26:30) turn.
* **ROWS 2–4:** dec neck edge.
ROWS 5–11 (11:13): dec neck edge on alt rows. *(17:19:22sts)*
Work further 3(5:5) rows.
Cast (bind) off. *
Place centre 12(14:14)sts on holder. Rejoin yarn to remaining sts at neck edge and knit to end. Work * to * again.

SLEEVES

Using 3¼mm (US 3) needles and C, cast on 36(36:40)sts. Work rows 1–14 as on back welt, inc each end of last row on size 2. *(36:38:40sts)*
Change to 4mm (US 6) needles and stocking (stockinette) stitch. Work rows 1–15 from border graph, inc each end of rows 5, 9 and 13. Change to M and cont incs on every foll 4th row to 52(58:62)sts. Cont without shaping until work measures 20(25:30)cm (8:10:12in). Place markers at each end of last row. Work further 4(6:6) rows. Cast (bind) off.

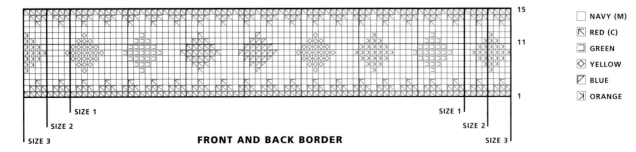

	NAVY (M)
◺	RED (C)
☐	GREEN
◈	YELLOW
◿	BLUE
⧄	ORANGE

SIZE 1   SIZE 1
SIZE 2   SIZE 2
SIZE 3   SIZE 3

FRONT AND BACK BORDER

r o o s t e r   s w e a t e r

NECKBAND

Join right shoulder seam. With RS facing and using 3¼mm (US 3) needles and M, pick up and knit 14(16:18)sts from side front neck, 12(14:14)sts from holder, 14(16:18)sts from side front neck, 3(4:3)sts from side back neck, 20(22:24)sts from holder and 3(4:3)sts from side back neck.
Work 7 rows in k2 p2 rib.
Change to C and work 6 rows in stocking (stockinette) stitch. Cast (bind) off loosely.

MAKING UP

Join left shoulder seam and neckband. Join side seams. Join sleeve seams to marker. Set in sleeves (see diagram on page 95), and stitch into place. Weave in any loose ends. Allow edges to curl (see photograph).

SIZES

	1	2	3
to fit years	1–2	3–4	5–6
actual size chest cm(in)	66(26)	76(30)	81(32)
back length cm(in)	33(13)	38(15)	44(17½)
sleeve seam cm(in)	20(8)	25(10)	30(12)

MATERIALS

Rowan Handknit DK Cotton 50g balls

navy (M)	4	5	6
red (C)	2	2	2
green	1	1	1
yellow	1	1	1
blue	1	1	1
orange	1	1	1

1 pair each 3¼mm (US 3) and 4mm (US 6) needles
Stitch holders

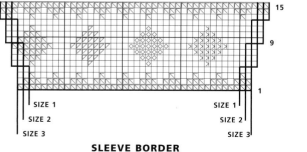

15	☐ NAVY (M)
9	◥ RED (C)
	⊐ GREEN
	◇ YELLOW
1	⊿ BLUE
	⋈ ORANGE

SIZE 1   SIZE 1
SIZE 2   SIZE 2
SIZE 3   SIZE 3

SLEEVE BORDER

l a d y b i r d c u s h i o n

SIZE
36cm (14in) square

MATERIALS
Rowan Cotton Glace 50g balls

red (M)	4
ecru (C)	1
black	1

36cm (14in) square cushion pad
3 buttons

1 pair 3¾mm (US 5) needles

TENSION (GAUGE)
23sts and 32 rows = 10cm (4in) square over stocking (stockinette) stitch using 3¾mm (US 5) needles.

ABBREVIATIONS
See page 95.

FRONT
Using M, cast on 83sts and work 44 rows in moss stitch.

ROW 45: using M, moss 30; using C, k23 (row 1 of motif); using M, moss 30.

ROWS 46–76: cont with motif from graph using stocking (stockinette) stitch and keep 30sts in moss stitch.

ROW 77: using M, moss 30, k23, moss 30.

ROWS 78–120: using M, moss stitch.
Cast (bind) off.

BACK
Using M, cast on 83sts. Work 60 rows in stocking (stockinette) stitch.

ROWS 61–63: k1 p1 rib.

Buttonhole

ROW 64: ✳ rib 20, cast (bind) off 1st ✳ 3 times, rib 20.

ROW 65: ✳ rib 20 yrn ✳ 3 times, rib 20.

ROWS 66–68: rib.
Cast (bind) off.
Make 2nd piece omitting buttonholes.

MAKING UP
Weave in any loose ends. Place back and front RS together making sure buttonhole back is underneath button back. Sew all four sides of cushion. Turn right side out. Sew on buttons.

ladybird blanket

TENSION (GAUGE)

23sts and 32 rows = 10cm (4in) square over stocking (stockinette) stitch using 3¾mm (US 5) needles.

BLANKET

Using M, cast on 151sts and work 8 rows in moss stitch (every row: *k1 p1* to last st, k1).

ROW 9: * using M, moss 6; using C, k23 (row 1 of motif) * 5 times; using M, moss 6.

ROWS 10–40: work motifs keeping moss borders correct.

ROW 41: using M, knit.

ROW 42–48: using M, moss stitch.

Repeat rows 9–48 six more times. Cast (bind) off. Weave in any loose ends.

SIZE

66cm (26in) wide and 90cm (35½in) long

MATERIALS

Rowan Cotton Glace 50g balls

red (M)	5
ecru (C)	4
black	3

1 pair 3¾mm (US 5) needles

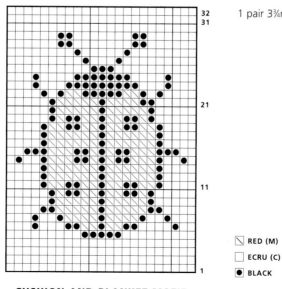

◣	RED (M)
☐	ECRU (C)
●	BLACK

CUSHION AND BLANKET MOTIF

ladybird hat

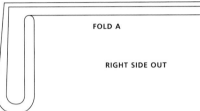

SEW TOGETHER CAST ON AND
CAST (BOUND) OFF EDGES

FOLD A

RIGHT SIDE OUT

SIZE

to fit years	2-3

MATERIALS

Rowan Cotton Glace 50g balls

red (M)	1
black (C)	1

1 pair 5mm (US 8) needles

TENSION

20sts and 24 rows = 10cm (4in) square over stocking (stockinette) stitch using 5mm (US 8) needles.

ABBREVIATIONS

See page 95.

BACK

Using C, cast on 46sts and work 20 rows in stocking (stockinette) stitch.
Change to M and work as folls:–
ROW 1: using M, k14 k2tog k6, k2C, using M, k6 k2tog k14. *(44sts)*
ROWS 2–36: follow graph. Cast (bind) off.

FRONT

Make as back.

ANTENNA (2)

Using C, cast on 15sts. Work 16 rows in stocking (stockinette) stitch. Cast (bind) off.

MAKING UP

Fold antenna in half, cast (bound) off edge to cast on edge, RS outside. Slipstitch together, having the cast on edge slightly proud (see diagram above).
Fold in half again and firmly stitch the cast on edge to the half fold A. Attach one end to back hat at marker. Repeat for other antenna. Placing RS of front and back hats together, sew M part of hat. Turn RS out and flat seam C part. Allow C to form a roll hem.

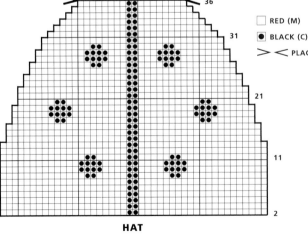

□ RED (M)
● BLACK (C)
>< PLACE MARKER

HAT

94

pattern information

ABBREVIATIONS

The following abbreviations are those most commonly used in all the patterns. Where individual patterns have special abbreviations, these are explained at the beginning of the patterns. Where cast (bound) off stitches are given in the middle of a row, the last stitch of the cast (bind) off is always included in the instructions that follow.

alt = alternate

beg = beginning

C = contrast colour

cont = continue

dec = decrease by knitting the next 2 stitches together

foll = following

inc = increase by knitting into the front and back of the next stitch

k = knit

k1, p1 rib = (on even number of sts) every row: *k1, p1* to end
= (on odd number of sts) row 1: *k1, p1* to last, k1, row 2: k1 *k1, p1* to end

k2tog = knit next 2 stitches together

k2togb = knit next 2 stitches together through back of loops

k3tog = knit next 3 stitches together

M = main colour

m1 = make stitch by picking up yarn before next stitch and knitting into the back of made loop.

moss stitch = (on even number of sts) row 1: *k1, p1* to end, row 2: *p1, k1* to end
= (on odd number of sts) every row: *k1, p1* to last st, k1

p = purl

p2tog = purl next 2 stitches together

p2togb = purl next 2 stitches together through back of loops

p3tog = purl next 3 stitches together

patt = pattern

psso = pass slipped stitch over

rem = remaining

sk = slip next stitch knitwise

sl = slip next stitch

sp = slip next stitch purlwise

stocking (stockinette) stitch =
row 1: knit, row 2: purl

st (s) = stitch (es)

tog = together

yb = yarn back

yf = yarn forward

yrn = yarn around needle

** = repeat enclosed instructions the number of times indicated by numeral

( ) = brackets refer to larger size (s). Where only one figure is given it refers to all sizes

NEEDLE SIZES

Here is a table showing international sizes.

Metric	British	American
2¾mm	12	2
3mm	11	3
3¼mm	10	3
3¾mm	9	5
4mm	8	6
4½mm	7	7
5mm	6	8

HOW TO DO A TENSION SQUARE

Please check your own tension before you start. Some people find that they need to use a smaller needle when knitting cotton. Cast on at least 30sts and work at least 40 rows. Measure only the sts given (e.g. 22sts by 28 rows) to check your tension. Remember that one stitch too many or too few over 10cm (4in) can spoil your work. If you have too many stitches, change to a larger needle, or if you have too few, change to a smaller size, and try again until the tension square is correct. Note: yarns from different manufacturers may not knit to the tensions given.

IMPORTANT NOTE ON COLOUR KNITTING

Most of the designs in this book involve different-coloured motifs or shapes worked into the main knitting. In the patterns you are advised to use 'block knitting' or 'intarsia' technique. This means using separate balls of contrast colours, or shorter lengths wound around bobbins, but NOT carrying the main yarn across the back of the section. This is partly to avoid bulky knitting, but mainly to avoid pulling in the work, which reduces the size of the motifs and distorts the knitting, even changing its size. Please work these areas with separate yarns, twisting them at the colour change to avoid holes forming.

CARE INSTRUCTIONS

Steam your knitting lightly by using a warm iron over a damp cloth. Never let the iron come directly in contact with the knitting. Ease the knitting into shape, or block it out with pins until the steam has completely dried off. For washing instructions, see the yarn's ball bands.

HOW TO FIT SLEEVE

Sleeve must fit in squarely.

Fit **A** to **A**,
B to **B**
C to **C**.

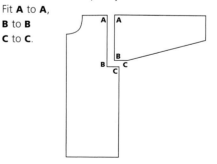

acknowledgements

Thanks to Gill and Eva for their expert pattern checking and support. Thanks to Joey for his beautiful photographs – and for working with children and animals! Thanks to Luise for the clear, modern, beautiful book design. Thanks to Kate Kirby and Kate Haxell for all their support and for making the book the way it is. Thanks also to all involved for the fun we had shooting this book. Thanks to Tim for the poem on page 10. Thanks to Olivia and Ellis, Toby's friends, and to my little Toby himself, and to all the other models – you look fab! Thanks too to Richmond Park and the Ragged Museum for letting us use them as locations and also to Godstone Farm for their hospitality and camera-friendly animals.

suppliers

Zoë Mellor can be contacted at: 15 Montpelier Place, Brighton, East Sussex BN1 3BF. Tel: 01273-710610

SUPPLIERS OF ROWAN YARNS

Australia
Rowan at Sunspun
185 Canterbury Road
Canterbury
Victoria 3126
Tel: 03 9830 1609

Canada
Diamond Yarn
9697 St Laurent
Montreal
Quebec H3L 2N1
Tel: 514 388 6188

Diamond Yarn (Toronto)
155 Martin Ross
Unit 3
Toronto
Ontario M3J 2L9
Tel: 416 736 6111

UK
Rowan Yarns
Green Mill Lane
Holmfirth
West Yorkshire HD7 1RW
Tel: 01484 681881

Mail order: Selfridges
400 Oxford Street
London W1A 1AB
Tel: 020 7328 3856

USA
Westminster Fibres Inc.
5 Northern Boulevard
Amherst
New Hampshire 03031
Tel: 603 886 5041/5043